Resources and Decisions

The Leonardo Scholars

University of Wisconsin

Duxbury Press

North Scituate, Massachusetts

A Division of Wadsworth Publishing Company, Inc.
Belmont, California

Duxbury Press

A DIVISION OF WADSWORTH PUBLISHING COMPANY, INC.

Resources and Decisions was edited and prepared for composition by Gail Stewart. Interior design was provided by Dorothy Booth and the cover was designed by Patricia Sustendal.

L.C. Cat. Card No.: 74-84834
ISBN 0-87872-086-3

PRINTED IN THE UNITED STATES OF AMERICA

1 2 3 4 5 6 7 8 9 10 — 79 78 77 76 75

Contents

LESLIE DIENES
Department of Geography

Foreward   ix
Preface   xi
Acknowledgments

CHAPTER ONE
Resource Policy in Perspective   1

Five Challenges of Long-range Planning   1
The Time and Space Dimensions   3
The Global Dimension   6
The National Dimension   7
The Concept of Points of No Return   9
Buying Time: Ignorance Is No Excuse   9
References   10

CHAPTER TWO
Constraints of Social Organization
On Decision-Making   12

Criticizing with Hindsight   12
Society and Policy   13
Biophysical Constraints   14
Social Myths and Values   15
Institutions   19
References   21

CHAPTER THREE
Estimates, Projections, and Forecasts   23

Estimates   23
Nonrenewable Resources: Distribution   24
Nonrenewable Resources: Estimates of Quantity   25
Renewable Resources: Estimating Wild Population   29
Renewable Resources: Estimating Domesticated Populations   30
The Dynamics of Estimating   31
Projections and Forecasts   33
How Forecasts Are Used   36
A Case Study: The National Power Survey   37
References   38

CHAPTER FOUR
Models: Finding Alternative Futures   41

What is a Model?   41
Characteristics of Models   42

Trend Projections   44
Econometric Models   45
Scenario-Building and Simulation Modeling   51
Some Concluding Comments on Models   57
References   58

CHAPTER FIVE
Faustian and Other Bargains   60

Risks and Payments   60
The Unseen Costs of Nuclear Power   62
The Faustian Bargain   63
Technology's Other Bargains   66
Are We Ready to Bargain?   68
References   70

CHAPTER SIX
Resource Use in Conflict   71

The Dilemma   71
Oil Tankers and Marine Fisheries   72
Wheat Versus Coal   74
Looking Beyond the Dilemma   82
References   82

CHAPTER SEVEN
Conservation of Materials and Energy   85

Energy and Materials Flow   85
Opportunities for Energy Conservation   90
Improved Space Heating and Cooling Practices   90
Improved Transportation Systems   92
Recycling   99
Opportunities for Materials Recycling   100
A Practical Example   107
The Waste Problem   110
Why the Waste?   110
References   114

CHAPTER EIGHT
The Bigger They Come . . .   117

Consumer and Producer Attitudes   117
Economies of Scale   119
Effects of Bigness on Competitors   123
Alternative Sources of Energy   124
Maintaining Diversity   128
References   129

CHAPTER NINE
Small Steps to Solve Big Problems   132

The Incremental Effect   132

A Case in Point: Reduction of Pollution from Stack Emissions   133
References   139

CHAPTER TEN
Can There Be Equity?   *142*

Ideal Survival   142
Can There Be Equity?   143
Beyond the Minimal Requirements   146
The Ethical Dimension   147
Seeking the Fine Line   148
The Role of the Individual   150
Optimism and Pessimism   151
References   152

The Leonardo Scholars   154
Guest Participants   156
Index   160

Foreword

This volume, *Resources and Decisions*, represents a major experiment in inter-disciplinary effort at the University of Wisconsin–Madison.

In the past we have repeatedly stressed the need for interdisciplinary scholarship, yet we have tended to underestimate the amount of effort and time required to produce really integrated analysis. Interdisciplinary work from closely related fields has been possible and productive, but rarely have we systematically brought together scholars from natural sciences, social sciences, and the humanities in a single effort.

The Institute for Environmental Studies at our university recommended to me that a faculty group be convened to give seven months' undivided attention to one of the major issues of our time; that is, an analysis of trends in resource supply and consumption in the United States, the institutions we have generated to deal with these trends, and how resource policy might be realigned. In the fall of 1972 I appointed the first Leonardo Scholars at our institution—five professors, representing the fields of anthropology and history, law, biochemistry, political science, and nuclear engineering, and the environmental reporter of the *Milwaukee Journal*. While we were concerned with selecting participants with expertise in matters of resources, we also were concerned with appointing individuals who could bring the skills and wisdom of their disciplines into the interdisciplinary arena. In mounting this effort, we were fortunate to have support from the National Science Foundation, from our own Graduate School, and from the *Milwaukee Journal*.

Resources and Decisions is the initial and perhaps most obvious product of the group's intensive effort. However, also emerging from the seminar is a new approach to courses and research by the participating professors, as well as in-depth coverage of the broader resource questions in the *Milwaukee Journal*.

This book presents the combined efforts of individuals from different back-grounds. The chapters reflect the contribution of all members of the seminar and thus do not have individual authors. It is intentional that none of the scholars wrote as they would to an audience of departmental colleagues. It is a truly inter-disciplinary work, and we believe a contribution of national significance.

We are pleased that its publication at this time helps us mark the 125th anniversary of the founding of the University of Wisconsin–Madison, for it carries one step further the intention of those who, in establishing this institution, sought to bring the benefits of the highest scholarship to all the people.

Edwin Young
Chancellor
University of Wisconsin–Madison

Preface

In August of 1973, after a seven-month study of selected natural resource policies in the United States, the six members of the Leonardo Seminar submitted their report and formally disbanded. The essence of their report was that U.S. policy on natural resources was in urgent need of review. The nation, for a number of reasons, seemed to be moving from a longstanding position of abundance, surplus, and low prices in essential commodities to one of relative shortages and high prices. Moreover, international politics, U.S. economic interests, rising affluence in the United States and other developed nations, increasing world population, and exponential growth in consumption suggested that shortages would be of a persistent rather than temporary nature.

Within a few months, the seminar's findings were dramatically illustrated. The outbreak of war in the Middle East and the subsequent cutoff of Arabian oil supplies to western countries, although not as directly related to American energy shortages as other factors, threw the United States into a state of "energy crisis" and aggravated already developing material shortages.

Reactions, both public and private, to the shortage situation underlined the importance of a central seminar conclusion: that the United States could no longer afford to substitute short-term crisis solutions for well-planned, long-term policies that would give full consideration to economic, social, and environmental effects and to impacts on institutional and international relations.

This book presents issues that six men judged crucial to future resource policy. It is not expected that their thoughts will solve resource policy problems. Problem-solving is a bargaining process, not a monologue. It is hoped, however, that the book will offer fresh insights and new perspectives on resource issues now before the public.

The seminar focused on three representative resources: copper, a nonrenewable material; wheat, a renewable resource; and energy, the lifeblood of all material production. The study began with copper. Each seminar member pursued in depth some aspect of its processing and consumption — the legal issues of mining rights, the energy demands of smelting, or the interplay between the copper market and the government stockpile. Whether through legal case studies, natural and social sciences, literature, or direct interviews, each scholar pursued his own discipline.

The study was supplemented by the testimony of invited guests, either experts in their fields at universities or men active in public agencies or industry. The guests' contributions were often as valuable for the points of view they offered as for the objective data presented.

Copper was a good topic for beginning such a study. Its exploitation is not as complex as that of some other resources. Yet it involves all the elements critical to decisions on the extraction, marketing, and use of any natural resource. These factors include estimates of world and national supply, processing methods, pricing systems, essential uses, substitute materials, energy costs, pollution and disposal problems, recycling potentials, corporate structure of the industry, and important areas of government control and intervention.

From detailed discussions of copper, wheat, and energy came the focus for the larger issues discussed in this volume: that social organizations, particularly natural resource institutions (public and private), are limited in their abilities to direct policy change; that forecasts of supply and demand require critical scrutiny; that hasty decisions involving long-term policies can be "bad bargains"; that conflicts over resource usage are inevitable if material and energy shortages persist; that new patterns of material and energy consumption must be encouraged in order to conserve these commodities; that reliance on monopolistic "economies of scale" results in reduction of alternative sources of energy and material; and that change in policy is more often accomplished by numerous small steps rather than through sweeping and often ineffectual bans.

Finally, not to be overlooked was the constantly posed issue of ethics. Does the United States have a responsibility to consider the well-being of poorer, less powerful nations and for that matter the poor within its own boundaries when formulating a resource policy? If so, what, ideally, should that responsibility be?

One question arose repeatedly, yet was not satisfactorily resolved by the seminar: which costs of resource production should be included in the price of a commodity and which should be paid by the public in non-monetary forms such as environmental degradation and social misery? Until now America's resource wealth has enabled her to skirt this issue. But as this nation moves from a period of longstanding abundance to one of relative scarcity, unresolved issues of pricing policy must be confronted, including the questions:

1. Do current prices of energy or materials truly reflect the social and economic costs of production?

2. Is our reluctance to reuse or conserve materials at least partly the result of special incentives and benefits given to the producers of virgin natural resources?

3. Can the public interest be protected by present fragmented, often competing, panels of regulation, control, and review?

4. Can present forms of public regulation, whose responsibilities are confined to national or state boundaries, protect the public interest in a world where commerce and technical systems are international in scope?

A major conclusion to be drawn from all this question-raising is that no single principle of pricing, rationing, or resource distribution is at work in the United States. Although many producers often state that their problems would vanish if "free market systems" or "free enterprise" were permitted to function without interference, these same producers actively support and openly lobby for public interventions, such as taxing policy and import controls, that benefit them.

It appears that the U.S. economy is a structure based on intervention upon intervention, rule upon rule, and exception upon exception, to the extent that pricing policy eludes comprehension. Against this background, arguments between "free market" proponents and "interventionist" proponents seem unrelated to the real world. Nonetheless, the debate implies a choice between two extremes: a highly regulated market or unfettered private control of commerce.

We believe that totalitarianism is approached with the achievement of either ideal. On the one hand would be government control over production and distribution with the use of commodities decided not by individual tastes and needs, but along lines of national security and purpose. On the other hand would be unrestrained private commerce with its tendency to concentrate the control of international resources into fewer, ever more powerful hands.

In the underdeveloped two-thirds of the world, the central resource policy question is basic: how to extend acceptable levels of health, nutrition, shelter, and opportunity to millions of miserably poor people, thereby building a foundation from which they might invent their own futures.

For industrially sophisticated societies such as the United States, the central resource policy question seems to be how to preserve personal freedom and choice in a world in which it is becoming imperative to restrain environmentally damaging economic activity, conserve natural resources, yet satisfy the needs of all individuals.

The present system of economics in the United States, and in most of the world, stems from the operation of a single principle: pressure politics. This system has failed in meeting either goal, that of adequate supplies or that of environmental protection. It seems reasonable therefore to suggest striving for an ideal economy in which (a) producers of commodities pay for the identifiable social and environmental costs of production and pass such costs on to consumers, and (b) public social policies offer every citizen adequate nutrition, shelter, personal safety, health care, and education.

This book suggests that there are good reasons to aim for the ideal and there are means available for approaching it.

Acknowledgments

The Leonardo Scholars wish to thank the guest participants who spoke with the seminar.* We also thank graduate students Gerald J. Lawson, William L. Ford, Kenneth H. Pischer, Robert J. Griffin, and Jonathan Phipps for their research efforts; Jane E. Gaines for her secretarial assistance; and Jean M. Lang and Dennis L. Fisher for their editorial work. In addition, thanks go to Reid A. Bryson, director of the Institute for Environmental Studies, who conceived of the Leonardo Seminar, and to John E. Ross, associate director, who moved this book to its completion.

Finally, we are grateful to the funding agencies for their financial support: the National Science Foundation, Division of Research Applied to National Needs; the University of Wisconsin Graduate School; The Journal Company; and the Dupont Corporation.

* Guest participants are listed on page 156.

1.   Resource Policy In Perspective

Any examination of resource policy begins with certain implicit concerns and assumptions. The concerns are our assumed obligations to the human species and to the quality (as opposed to *quantity*) of human life now and in the future. These concerns are based on an underlying assumption that survival of the human species and improvement of the human condition are things that have to be consciously worked at and that efforts toward these ends must be made despite the possibility of unexpected and often unwanted consequences. This in turn involves an assumption that survival and improvement in the quality of life on either a national or a planetary scale will ultimately involve drastic changes in present trends, policies, and value systems.[1]

Five Challenges of Long-range Planning

As demands on world resources expand daily, man's future survival at some level beyond mere animal existence depends increasingly on the long-range planning that is done today. Critical to long-range plans are decisions regarding what have been called the four "interlocking variables whose unsatisfactory management threatens our options" — peace, population, pollution, and resource policy making.[2,3] A fifth challenge to man's long-range plans is the equitable distribution of resources at the national and international levels.[4]

The issues of peace and population will not be discussed in detail in this volume, but we take it as a premise that, in view of the finiteness of the spaceship Earth, the achievement of a reasonably healthy and stabilized world population at or below the present level (3.8 billion, 1972) is a desirable goal that is in need of much wider acceptance. Unfortunately, world population probably will move to much higher and unstable levels. And as world population increases, international efforts to promote general health and well-being will become more difficult. It may be that by the time all the options for population control have been thoroughly assessed, some options will have slipped quietly away. Whether limitation of growth can be accomplished by humane means or whether it will result only from the inexorable operation of biological constraints remains to be seen.

In any case resource policies that promote both peace and population control should be encouraged. This statement is made in full awareness of the sensitive nature of the population issue. Nothing seems to be more the private concern of individuals than size of family; and population policies surely are the business of national rather than international governments. But biological realities of unrestrained population growth and finite Earth compel us all to discuss, broadcast, and confront this issue. Such efforts should be made always in the light of public scrutiny so that rights, values, and cultural uniqueness are not disregarded. Diversity is a necessity in maintaining stability in any biological system, including a human one.[5] It seems clear that no one solution exists for poulation questions. The solution, if there is one, likely will be a composite of diverse strategies, since the problem differs from place to place and from culture to culture.

Our major concerns in this book will be environmental pollution and resource policy, two closely related aspects of long-range planning. The term *natural resources* is used here to mean those biological or physical phenomena — *other than human beings themselves*[6] — that exist in nature and that humans can adapt to their own uses and purposes.[7] Natural resources, in fact, is a term that can be used *only* in relation to the purposes and choices of man.

Even when contemporary technology has not yet made the utilization of a resource practical, theoretical science can indicate the potentially important resources. The case of nuclear fusion is a good example. Science indicates that vast amounts of energy can be obtained by the controlled fusion of the hydrogen isotopes deuterium and tritium, but so far technology has not been able to produce a reactor.

There is a similar relation between science and technology in the pollution problem. Scientists can detect many environmental impacts from the processing and utilization of natural resources and can indicate possible ways to recover waste products. But it is up to the contemporary technologist to convert theory into practice, with the invention of feasible processes for preventing pollution or recycling waste products. In many cases, such as the control of suflfur dioxide emissions or the disposal of solid waste, options are open for treating the waste products as resources; but these options are not now economically self-sustaining, given the rules by which the market operates.

At this point human value decisions enter in. Value decisions initially were responsible for the vast effort to convert natural resources into commercially saleable — and sometimes incidentally polluting — products. For the health and well-being of future generations, as well as present health and welfare, human value decisions now will have to weigh the economics of pollution prevention, waste recovery, and conservation in general. We must seek an equitable balance in distributing the costs of the social and environmental side effects associated with resource utilizations, between present and future generations as well as among the various segments of our present society, national and international.

The five challenges of long-range planning — peace, population, pollution, resource policy, and equity in resource distribution — are all closely interwoven, but the problems of resource management and pollution management are practically inseparable. A crucial problem in resource and pollution policy is how to control technology by para-economic means[8] so as to optimize the production of useful material and to minimize the appearance of harmful or unnecessary products in a way that is compatible with the long-range goals of humanity. Definitions of "necessary," "unnecessary," and "harmful" as well as definitions of "the quality of life" may depend to some extent on time and place. But the definitions may be sharpened by objective tests of community health in terms of the levels of disease, malnutrition, infant mortality, obesity, excessive birth and death rates, emotional well-being, and many other criteria.

The Time and Space Dimensions

Meadows et al. in *The Limits to Growth* have graphically illustrated the idea that there are two dimensions to every man's world.[9] One is in space, the other is in time. In *space*, one may be concerned about self, family, community, culture, nation, or world. In *time*, one may be concerned about today, next week, the next few years, a lifetime, children or grandchildren's lifetime, or centuries, but seldom beyond. In this two-dimensional grid, long-range planners must not only understand the time dimension in relation to the process of exponential growth, but should also be concerned with the concept of humanity.

For long-range planners as well as others, the year 2000 is a convenient time-mark, even though it may be only psychological in effect. Just as January first is a time for making New Year's resolutions, the year 2000 marks both the beginning of a new century and a new millennium. The children or grandchildren who are one year old in 1975 will, in the year 2000, be twenty-six, possibly be married, possibly be parents, probably have made many of life's major decisions, and be facing about fifty years of life in the twenty-first century. What will it be like?

The first key to visualizing that world, as Meadows et al. point out, is an understanding of exponential growth and its implications.[10] Exponential growth can be expressed in terms of the time it takes a given population to double in number (*doubling time*). This rate in turn is a function of *percent annual increase* or percent increase for any other specified time unit. The relationship is shown in Table 1.1.

TABLE 1.1. Exponential Growth

Percent Annual Increase	Doubling Time
0.1%	700 years
0.2%	350 years
0.5%	139 years
1.0%	70 years
2.0%	35 years
3.0%	23 years
4.0%	18 years
6.0%	11+ years
8.0%	8+ years
10.0%	7 years

Many critical components of the resource policy question — GNP, population, resource consumption — have increased at annual rates in the range of 2 percent to 10 percent, with doubling times of 30, 20, or 10 years. It is clear that we are dealing with time dimensions measured in years or decades, and that we cannot afford to wait until the year 2000 to make our "New Century" or "New Millennium" resolutions.

While no one can predict with certainty what growth curves will do between now and the year 2000 (see Chapter 3 for discussion of forecasting), it is possible to chart the course of events during the past few decades and to see what has been happening in terms of exponential growth. In examining any curve of exponential growth *from an already large base* it always should be remembered that the growth *cannot continue* indefinitely. Eventually the questions become "When will the rate decrease?" "How much?" "At what rate?" "Why?" and "Should deliberate intervention be attempted?"

In terms of population growth, Japan, the United States, and India had percent annual increases of 1.0, 1.4, and 2.5 respectively for the period 1961-1968. During this same period the increases in the gross national product per capita were 9.9, 3.4, and 1.0 percent per year respectively. These figures are not very startling unless they are converted to doubling times and projected into the future (Table 1.2).

Probably the first thing that should be said about the numbers in Table 1.2 is that the doubling times are not predictions. They are merely an *indication* of what would happen if 1961-1968 rates were to *continue unchanged.* In the case of populations that are already large we have to recognize the urgency of a situation in which the population could double in only 28 years. In the case of developed nations where GNPs are *already large,* we have to ask whether the world can cope with the resource depletion and the pollution that further increases in GNP would imply. As Commoner[11] and others have pointed out, pollution is a function of both production level and pollution generation per unit of production (that is, technology). Thus, the developed nations should be particularly sensitive to the way in which western consumption habits, combined with population increase, could compound environmental degradation on a global scale.

Whether we consider population or GNP doubling times, we must realize that time is short. Mankind no longer has the luxury of unlimited time for adjustments and adaptation. Unlike biological evolution which tested the response of species to change over millions of years, cultural evolution tests mankind's ability to survive over mere decades. For example, in the United States, high rates of energy consumption combined with exponentially increasing rates of per capita use have created a doubling time of about 10 years for electrical energy. Some technologists foresee no serious difficulties in supporting a world population of 15 billion at United States consumption levels, providing that the world has an "essentially inexhaustible energy source."[12] These technologists also believe that "from what we now know, this source must be nuclear."[13] However, such implied rates of worldwide energy and material consumption cannot be sustained forever. There must be a serious search within the next few decades for cultural alternatives.

TABLE 1.2. Population and GNP Doubling Times in Three Countries

Region	Population 1968 (millions)	Population Doubling Time* 1961–1968	GNP 1968 (billions of dollars)	GNP per capita 1968 (dollars)	GNP per capita Doubling Time* 1961–1968	Projected GNP per capita in Year 2000 (1968 dollars)
Japan	101	70 years	$120	$1,190	7 years	$23,200
U.S.	201	50 years	$800	$3,980	20 years	$11,000
India	524	28 years	$ 52.4	$ 100	70 years	$ 140

*Data recalculated from Meadows et al. (1972), pp. 42–43.

Culture is flexible and its change can be rapid under the right circumstances. Margaret Mead's studies of New Guinea tribes, described in *Continuities in Cultural Evolution*,[14] illustrate this point well. In later chapters we will attempt to suggest where reasonable societal changes offer solutions for resource problems.

The Global Dimension

One of the most useful products of the entire space program was a colored blue, green, white, and brown photo of Earth as seen from an Apollo spaceship returning from the moon. The analogy of earth itself as a spaceship, finite in nature, with an essentially closed system, depending on the distant sun for life-giving energy, was brought home to millions of people. Similarly, the experience of traveling across a continent or between continents in a few hours by modern jet aircraft has taught us that the earth is not unlimited in extent.

Meanwhile modern communications media have made vivid the reality of global population problems. We have become aware of the existence of large blocks of population in underdeveloped countries with fertility that is still high despite inadequate nutrition. With a world population of 3.8 billion increasing at an annual rate of 2 percent, we realize the possibility of doubling our numbers in 35 years (Table 1.1) or reaching, by UN medium estimate, 6.5 billion people by the year 2000. Asia has over half of the world's current population and counts its residents in billions at 2.15. All other countries make up the remaining 1.6 billion. Africa and Latin America account for 0.36 and 0.30 billion respectively, but, like Asia, are expected to more than double their populations by year 2000. North America (United States and Canada), Europe, and the Soviet Union contribute their fractions as 0.23, 0.47, and 0.25 billion. None of the nations in this group is expected to double in population by the year 2000 and many have present doubling times of over a century (Table 1.3).

Thus, from a global standpoint, Asia, Africa, and Latin America, which now contain 74 percent of the world population, may very well have 82 percent of the total by year 2000, while the United States, with 5.5 percent of the total now, may recede to 4.5 percent of the total.

Even though it may seem self-serving to raise the question, any attempt to deal with resource policy, conservation, pollution, or waste will need to consider whether it is physically possible or desirable for the underdeveloped parts of Asia, Africa, and Latin America to adopt our rates of energy and material resource consumption. The United States has the dubious distinction of being a nation with a level of resource consumption that is vastly disproportionate to its population, which comprises only 6 percent of the world's people. In view of our own problems arising from an expansive technology, it would appear desirable that all countries (including the United States) aim for some level of resource use well below the current U. S. advertised "norm." A level of resource use that is directed toward basic needs would be in the interests of both underdeveloped and developed countries. On a global scale, a reasonable goal would be the achievement of population levels consistent with national food production or capability to trade for food.

TABLE 1.3. World Population, Mid–1972 and in Year 2000 by UN Medium Estimate (From Population Reference Bureau, Inc.)

Region	Population Mid–1972 (billions)	Estimate Year 2000 (billions)	Doubling Time at Present Rate (years)	Infant Mortality (per 1,000 live births first year)
Asia[a]	2.15	3.78	30	13–142
Africa	.36	.82	27	100–190
Latin America	.30	.65	25	40–90
Oceania[b]	.02	.035	35	16–22
Europe	.47	.57	99	12–20
USSR	.25	.33	77	24
U.S. & Canada	.23	.33	63	19
Total World	3.78	6.5	35	—

[a]Includes Japan with 0.1 billion people in 1972 and a doubling time of 58 years at present rate, and infant mortality rate of only 13 per 1,000 in first year.
[b]Includes Australia and New Zealand.

Food availability is a major resource policy problem because of its relation to human health and survival. One index of general health and nutrition is the number of infant deaths under one year of age per 1,000 live births. Generally, the better a nation's health and nutrition, the lower the infant mortality rate. The rate varies tremendously in various parts of the world, ranging from a minimum of about 12 per 1,000 in Sweden, Netherlands, and Japan, to about 19 in the United States, to about 140 in India and Pakistan, and to the highest levels of around 180 deaths per 1,000 live births in parts of Africa (Table 1.3). The higher mortality rates undoubtedly reflect the consequences of malnutrition in many cases.

Looking at the positive side of the global dimension, there are already many encouraging developments. The population problem has led to formation of the United Nations Fund for Population Activities and the designation of 1974 as World Population Year. Regional economic organization such as the Common Market has facilitated trade. Environmental awareness of the national level has increased awareness of the world environment, and the first United Nations Conference on the Human Environment was held in Stockholm during 1972. Modern communication coupled with previously unheard-of changes in cultural and economic boundaries have brought home the realization that we are all part of the "global village."

The National Dimension

Yet despite this heightened awareness of the global dimension, the United States, with only 5.5 percent of the world population, continues to consume much more energy, food, and nonrenewable resources than any other country in the world. Our consumption of natural gas is greater than all of the rest of the world combined (63 percent of the total). We produce 23 percent of the world's petroleum and use 33 percent of the world total. Our use of metals is also around 30 percent of the world total.[15]

Our caloric intake is the world's highest, at about 3,240 kilocalories per day per capita.[16] Our protein intake exceeds our requirements and includes far more animal protein than in any other country except New Zealand (72 grams versus 75 grams per person per day, respectively). Borgstrom has noted that the average animal protein consumption in the better fed parts of the world is 44 grams per day per person while among the vast numbers in the poorly fed regions the average is 8 to 9 grams per day per person.[17] Moreover, the daily intake has increased by about 8 grams per day during the 1960s in the better fed countries and has *decreased* by about 3 grams in the poorly fed countries. In general the poorly fed countries are the ones in which the population is increasing most rapidly.

Not only is there great disparity in food intake between the United States and the rest of the world, but there are also great differences here at home. Our average of 72 grams animal protein per day is less than the New Zealander's 75 grams because our average includes tens of millions who do not get a balanced diet and who have a protein intake that is deficient by 10 to 12 percent. According to Borgstrom, "U.S. surveys show that 30 – 40 million people have an income insufficient for procuring an adequate diet and about 10 million of these are so critically short of vital nutrients that they show signs of protein deficiency — in other words, malnutrition."[18] The fact that the U.S. index of infant mortality during the first year is 19 per 1,000 live births compared to 12 in Sweden, Netherlands, and Japan is a possible indication of malnutrition and poor medical care among a substantial fraction of our population.

Meanwhile the resource and energy consumption of the affluent fraction of our population has increased rapidly since 1940. As stated earlier, electrical energy usage has had a doubling time of about 10 years. Present plans for additional electrical power plants are based on an assumed 10-year doubling time. This rate results in part from increases in the present per capita usage of 8,937 kwh per year[19] and from an assumed increase in population. Any just resource policy or energy conservation decision will have to meet the reasonable expectations of the underprivileged fraction of our national population even while asking the affluent fraction to conserve or diminish their consumption.

Much of the "conspicuous consumption" in the United States is the result of aggressive advertising. A clear definition of basic requirements for human mental and physical health, as opposed to these unnecessary demands, is crucially needed.

While there are many problems that remain to be solved, there are also encouraging developments in the national dimension. The existing concepts of economic success are being challenged, and there is a widespread concern with environmental preservation. The enactments of the National Environmental Policy Act,[20] the Occupational Safety and Health Act,[21] the Clean Air Act,[22] and the Water Quality Act[23] all attest to the national will to preserve and maintain a healthful environment. Although all of these laws came under attack during the energy crisis, there still remains a rather widespread recognition of the fallacy of single-purpose planning. Finally, many interdisciplinary study groups have been organized and are developing approaches to world and national problems.

The Concept of Points of No Return

In early transatlantic flights there was always a problem of carrying enough fuel. Depending on wind and weather it could be calculated that up to a certain point the plane could change course and return to base. But beyond that point it would not have enough fuel to make it back, and might as well try for the goal. The point at which fuel became insufficient was known as the "point of no return." Similarly, an endangered species reaches the point of no return when its numbers become so small and so widely dispersed that breeding and reproduction fail to replace the animals that die or are killed.

A city, polluting the air and water and depleting the forests and soils within an ever-increasing radius around itself, also can reach a point of no return when it becomes impossible to maintain and service the center city. At that point, the city loses its power and influence. Many urban centers in the world are now in the position of absolute dependence on transportation lifelines and at the same time are suffering from severe pollution. In the past, city dwellers could migrate to a new location and begin a new period of growth. But with strict immigration quotas and guarded borders migration no longer seems to be the solution.

Somehow our technologists will have to develop monitoring devices to warn us before empty fuel tanks or crop failures push us to points of no return. And, since food is one of the most critical biological realities, every nation should attempt to balance the size of its population with its ability to produce or import a food supply.

Buying Time: Ignorance Is No Excuse

The reason for describing man's future in terms of the time dimension and in terms of points of no return is to emphasize that resource policy makers do not always have the luxury of generating last-minute solutions to problems that have been neglected until they are obvious to everyone. It appears likely that at the first signs of an energy crisis or a food crisis a culture that has known affluence will demand that affluence be maintained. If this demand is met at the expense of the nonrenewable reserves and at the expense of the earth's capacity to produce renewable resources, it will hasten the degradation of planetary carrying capacity for plants, animals, and the human species.

Furthermore, if demands for the maintenance of affluence, here defined as a superabundance of material goods, are made in a world in which millions are suffering from hunger and disease, the gap between developed and underdeveloped countries will widen. Moreover, global cooperation in finding solutions for the suffering populations will become even more difficult.

No one can predict with certainty when the mineral and fossil fuel supplies will be depleted. No one can predict when the incidence of famine will jump to 5 or 10 times its present rate. However, it is clear that the increase in world population and the increase in resource consumption are on a collision course. The present incidence of hunger and disease, as evidenced by infant mortality, for example, is already high enough to suggest a need for drastic change. But how many deaths by starvation must there be to elicit a sense of urgency? The evidence regarding present rates of population growth and resource consumption has led to grave doubts that these rates of increase can be maintained for more than a few decades; we believe it is necessary to take immediate action to bring the two factors into balance.

It is our opinion that the well-to-do nations, those nations whose people still live in an atmosphere of health and plenty, must bear the weight of responsibility both in reducing their own population growth and unnecessary consumption, and in aiding the less fortunate nations in finding solutions to their immediate problems. Anything that can be done now to slow population growth and to preserve the carrying capacity of the earth will have the effect of buying time that can be used to develop better management of the earth's resources. To plead ignorance now will be to ensure that ignorance will prevail later, when wisdom will be needed.

References

1. These concerns and assumptions stem from a relatively recent line of thought which began in the seventeenth century and which focused on man's capacity for improvement. The history of this thought is described by John A. Passmore in *The Perfectibility of Man* (London: Duckworth, 1970).

2. Committee on Resources and Man, National Academy of Sciences-National Research Council, *Resources and Man* (San Francisco: Freeman, 1969), p. ix.

3. Richard A. Falk, *This Endangered Planet: Prospects and Proposals for Human Survival* (New York: Random House, 1971), pp. 104-213.

4. Lester R. Brown, *World Without Borders* (New York: Random House, 1972), pp. 41-57.

5. The Institute of Ecology, *Man in the Living Environment* (Madison: University of Wisconsin Press, 1972), pp. 112-17.

6. Human beings specifically are excluded from this definition since we do not condone societies which base their economic organization on the treatment of human beings as natural resources to be exploited. Although outright slavery is no longer common, there are modern forms — compatible with and sustained by modern science, economics, and technology — which are slavery's functional equivalent. We cannot, by default or silence, fail to note that this violates a norm that we would prefer to see people defend and maintain.

7. One view of the uses and purposes that are regarded as suitable is expresed in Chapter 10 below. Chapter 5, below, on "Faustian and Other Bargains," delineates uses and purposes that should be precluded—or certainly postponed in any contemporary American natural resources decision.

8. By para-economic means we mean methods that attempt to affect economic decisions by appealing to value judgments. See the reference to Carl Madden in Chapter 10 below.

9. Donella H. Meadows, Dennis L. Meadows, Jørgen Randers, and William W. Behrens III, *The Limits to Growth* (New York: Universe, 1972), p. 19.

10. Ibid., pp. 25-44.

11. Barry Commoner, *The Closing Circle* (New York: Knopf, 1971). pp. 45-46.

12. A. P. Weinberg and R. P. Hammond, "Global Effects of Increased Use of Energy," *Proceedings of the Fourth International Conference on the Peaceful Uses of Atomic Energy*, Geneva, Switzerland (jointly sponsored by the United Nations and the International Atomic Energy Commission, September 6-16, 1971) vol. 1, p. 174.

13. Ibid., p. 184.

14. Margaret Mead, *Continuities in Cultural Evolution* (New Haven: Yale University Press, 1964), p. 334.

15. Meadows et al., *Limits to Growth*, pp. 55-60.

16. Georg Borgstrom, *The Hungry Planet: The Modern World at the Edge of Famine* (New York: Macmillan, 1972), p. 32. A kilocalorie, also called "kilogram calorie" or "large calorie," is the unit which measures the energy produced by food when oxidized in the body. It is the amount of energy, in heat, required to raise the temperature of one kilogram of water one degree centigrade at a pressure of one atmosphere.

17. Georg Borgstrom, "Food Plants," in "Public Policy Toward Environment 1973: A Review and Appraisal," *Annals New York Academy of Sciences* 216: 106 (May 18, 1973). Animal protein is used here as the standard for nutrition since plant proteins, particularly wheat and corn, tend to be deficient in certain amino acids, such as lysine, that are found in animal protein.

18. Borgstrom, "Food Plants," p. 106.

19. *Statistical Yearbook of the Electric Utility Industry for 1972* Edison Electric Institute (New York: 1973), Table 7S, p. 13.

20. National Environmental Policy Act of 1969, 42 U.S.C. § § 4321, 4331-4335, 4341-4347 (1970).

21. Occupational Safety and Health Act of 1970, 84 Stat. § 1590 [codified in scattered sections of 5, 15, 18, 29, 42, 49, U.S.C. (1970)].

22. Clean Air Act, 77 Stat. §392 (1963), *as amended* 42 U.S.C. § § 1857-1857(1), 1858-1858(a) (1970).

23. Water Quality Act of 1965, 79 Stat. §903 (1965), *as amended* 33 U.S.C. § §1151 et seq. (1970).

2. Constraints of Social Organization On Decision-Making

In a certain sense, the issue posed here is that posed before the whole world: what decisions should human beings make today about resource uses that will be pursued in the future? We shall not answer this difficult question directly. Instead, we shall discuss the elements of a procedure for making natural resources decisions, pointing up considerations that are sometimes neglected in the making of resource policy.

For example, the discussion of energy policy in Chapter 5, "Faustian and Other Bargains," suggests that it would be wise to hold off for a while on public commitments to the breeder reactor and other forms of nuclear power development. However, before making such a decision, it is necessary to consider as well the adverse consequences that might accompany a heavier reliance on coal — which is a major alternative to nuclear power — unless one imagines far more drastic reductions in energy consumption than most commentators now anticipate.

Criticizing with Hindsight

A discussion of these and other resource issues needs an historical perspective. It is commonly suggested that decision-makers in the past could have done better, knew that they could have done better, and carelessly neglected to do so. There is no doubt that most of our present environmental problems are a function of the high rates of consumption of the advanced industrial societies. It is equally clear that these rates of consumption are the results of human decisions made in the past. But we should guard against the temptation to show 20-20 hindsight. Criticisms of earlier decisions are superficial unless those who make them are prepared to indicate what policies would have been wiser, and could have been conceived and executed, in the world as it then was. For example, should the midwestern hardwood forests have been sacrificed for farmland? Should access to cheap hydroelectric power have been facilitated by a Tennessee Valley Authority and a Bonneville Power Administration? Should the United States have encouraged the family farm, or not?

When looking at U.S. consumption or exploitation rates in retrospect, two points should be remembered. The first is one advanced by advocates of economic growth.[1] If the United States had not experienced the rates of economic growth and consumption that it did, then either (a) inequalities within the advanced industrial societies would be much greater than they now are or (b) the inequalities might be no greater, but everyone would be much worse off in a material sense. In addition, *we have to ask to what degree social conflict in the United States has been mitigated by the past high level of material consumption.* Could a *poor* United States have put an end to slavery? Could a poor United States have developed a widespread system of secondary and higher education? Could a poor United States have avoided severe battles between the working classes and their employers?

The second point is that decision-makers in the past presumably acted on the basis of the knowledge they then had, and can be criticized only if we can show that they could reasonably have had other knowledge which they casually neglected to get.

Careful consideration of these points suggests the need for similar restraint in criticizing current resource policy decisions. It is apparent that many questions being debated in the 1970s are not unlike questions raised in the past. How, then, should we judge to what extent it is prophetic — and to what extent merely fatuous — to urge that people today put aside all conflicts and hostilities in order to concentrate on saving the human race from eco-suicide? To what extent should national environmental policy in the United States take explicit account of the problems of distributing the national product? How should we view the "rights" or the "capacity" of decision-makers to intervene in private decisions? How should environmental issues be weighed against the rich-poor relationship at the global level?

Society and Policy

Whatever answers one might offer, it is apparent that goodness or badness of natural resources policies is a function of social organization. Thus, if the quality of natural resources decisions is to be improved, it will be absolutely essential to give more thought to the reciprocal relation between social organization and decisions about natural resources exploitation.

If this proposition is rephrased as an equation, social organization may be taken as the input (or independent variable) and a given pattern of resource use may be viewed as the outcome (or dependent variable). For example, if a democratic society decides through its elected representatives in the legislative branch to restrict the size of companies that can exploit a resource, such as limiting the size of corporate farms, this limitation will influence the way in which the resource is managed, its consumer price, and consequently its use.

But it is possible to reverse the equation and make social organization the dependent variable and the consequence of some earlier natural resource decisions. As an illustration, consider the decision of early settlers near the village of Pike Creek in southeastern Wisconsin.[2] The surrounding lands were as yet unsurveyed by the federal government, and no lawful entry or claim of right could be made under existing law. Yet the settlers wanted to exploit the lands. They created their own authority, the Pike River Claimants Union, to determine priority and settle disputes over boundaries of land claims among the inhabitants. Once the decision to utilize the resource was made, a social organization was devised to accommodate that decision.

For a more complex example, consider that many serious students of environmental policy today recommend the allocation of resources by the use of a "free market," which allows prices to find their natural levels. The reasoning is that if people are forced, as the free market presumably would force them, to absorb the costs of their own impact on the environment, they would alter their behaviors rather than pay the costs. Apart from any evaluation of whether this would have the desired environmental effect, we should recognize that we are talking about a new social institution, the workability of which is yet untested. The free market, in the sense envisioned by classical economic theory, has probably never existed. And it certainly has never existed for long on a large scale. There is no history of a solely economic system in which the aggregate of blind individual choices produced an overall social allocation through the oscillations of the price system. We have no history of a time in which there was a sufficient number of buyers and sellers, each possessing sufficient information, that no one (or no small group) could dictate price. Nor do we have any history of a period in which government did not, in one way or another, intervene in the market mechanism.[3] Accordingly, free market proposals must be regarded as proposals for innovation. And, considering the actual web of restraints working against it, a free market would introduce the most remarkable uncertainties into the industrial picture.[4]

In short, an imagined policy such as the creation of a totally free market will not be adopted merely because it has been judged "good" or "rational" or "desirable" by some single criterion. Nor, if adopted, will all of the policy's results inevitably be good. Adverse side effects are to be considered quite seriously, and decisions about natural resources should be guided by the maxim "first, do no harm." The possibility that unexpected outcomes will follow a policy decision cannot legitimately be ignored. They cannot be ignored if only because natural resource decisions — despite the technocratic language in which we express them — are exercises of power in which a group A seeks to compel group B to do what A prefers, and what B would not do except for A's intervention.

Because resource policy decisions are political decisions, they are not made in a vacuum. Rather they are molded by a matrix consisting of a people's biophysical setting, their social myths and values, and their formal institutions.

Biophysical Constraints

Social organization is constrained, in a very fundamental sense, by the biophysical environment in which it operates. This is self-evident and at the same time mysterious. Montesquieu recognized this constraint and developed from it a political theory which emphasized climate as a determinant of human action.[5] Awareness of the biophysical setting is also apparent in the environmental determinism of Ellsworth Huntington.[6] For example, when scarcity of rainfall (America's high plains) or cold temperatures (Iceland) shorten the growing season, people use the land for pasturing cattle and sheep rather than for cultivating crops. This choice of economy in turn influences the population's density and its way of life. People express some recognition of biophysical effects when they speak of the way in which Soviet agriculture "has to" respond to the extreme cold of the Soviet Union as well as to the constraints of Marxist-Leninist theory. People also recognize the extreme heat and aridity of Arizona when they insist on federal water subsidies to make cotton-growing practical.

Despite our recognition of the biophysical setting, our understanding of its specific connections to social behavior is rather muddled. We know with certainty that reduction of food supply for population X will cause some kind of strain within that population. But we do not know to what extent people will reorganize their society to share the reduced ration, or to what extent there will be simple abandonment and loss of hope.

For this reason we cannot be very certain about what must happen to social organization under hypothesized conditions. We surely can say that if population increases while food resources remain at static level, then the food per capita will decline. But does this mean that everyone's food consumption will drop? Does it mean that some people's consumption will go up while other people's goes down? What additional proportion — above the normal number — will die of starvation? And in what ways would the social relations change if these physical relations change?

Crude generalization from studies of isolated human populations, or from animal populations, can suggest answers. But they are no more credible answers than our present guesses. The best we can do now is to recognize that biophysical constraints are at once self-evident — in that we recognize them — and mysterious — in that we cannot predict their effects.

Social Myths and Values

People in groups respond differently, at different times, to challenges that appear similar. One explanation for this is that the actions of any given group are dominated by the group's unique social myths and values. By *social myths* we mean the received doctrines that people use to interpret, and to impose psychological and intellectual order upon, the world in which they live. These doctrines, or myths, explain what happens and why. They also provide moral criteria that people use as indicators of what they themselves ought to do. Myths may be less coherent than the beliefs usually called *values*, but they are very convincing to their adherents and are likely to be retained even if factual support for them is weak or nonexistent, or they are patently contradicted by empirical knowledge.

Myths and values do not have the same potency individually as they have when grouped in patterns or complexes. Collectively, myths and values are a strong force. Thus a given group of people in a given situation will have a pattern of social myths and values that they impose upon all their actions. It is their overall interpretation of the world and may be held consciously, semiconsciously, or perhaps even unconsciously.

As an illustration, consider the question of power in society. Some societies believe that power (the control of some human beings by other human beings) is evil, and can and should be restrained. In other societies, power is thought to be evil, but not easily restrained. And in still other societies, the question of power's evil does not exist. It is assumed that every rational man should and does quest after power.

As another example, the citizens of city X may commonly assume that any randomly chosen public official is taking graft if one could but locate the evidence to prove it. However, in city Y nearby, with a slightly different culture, the general assumption will be that public officials *may* be stealing but there is a good chance that they are not.

It is revealing to look at the myths held by educated people at various times in history. Very likely, most educated people prior to the twentieth century took for granted the intervention of preternatural or supernatural forces in human affairs. It was normal for the best-educated people in Greece at the time of Plato, Pericles, or Aristotle, or in Rome at the time of Julius Caesar or Cicero, to believe in and consult oracles. It was equally normal for an educated man in the time of Martin Luther to speak seriously of the perils of "this world with Demons filled." In contrast, the ruling elites and educated classes of the advanced industrial states today purport to believe in "rationality," "science," and "planning."[7] Yet these methods may actually serve as contemporary myths and values.

The very existence of this volume represents a manifestation of modern myths and values. It is not a "fact" that the thought and attention given to a problem by trained intellectuals is a positive contribution to human welfare, but an act of faith that it is so. A part of this same modern myth and value pattern is the belief that quantification represents a form of knowledge superior to other forms on which human actions might be reasonably based. Three dimensions of this myth are expressed in the following maxims.

(1) *On any given phenomenon, a quantitative statement is better than a qualitative statement.* You "know more" when you convert an inelegant, complex statement full of subtleties into an elegant simplified statement in which the subtleties are reduced.

(2) *The conversion into quantitative form is preferable even if, by making it, you sacrifice much of the phenomenon that you are trying to understand.* Thus, it is better to convert "law and order" into the number of arrests made by police, wealth into gross national product, or equity into comparative infant mortality rates. There is no doubt that many of these quantifications are extremely important methods for our knowledge and bases for choice, but they are often improperly used as the *equivalent* of knowledge or bases for choice. One could argue that such a use serves a ritualistic function of assurance and justification (*not* of verification), much as witchcraft did in the European and American past (and still does in some parts of European and American society and in other areas of the world).[8]

(3) On any important problem, those aspects that can be quantified should be given preference to those aspects that cannot be quantified. This last aspect is well illustrated by Guy Benveniste's account of decisions about the U.S. course in Vietnam.

> Facts about local attitudes, political commitments, and culture are not as easily understood and often seem to bend to fit military or economic facts. It is those who have the more "hard-nosed" facts who find access to the president and to the inner councils where decisions are made. Yet the evidence indicates that the hard-nosed facts tend to be in error, that the expected reactions of the "enemy" are systematically downgraded. In the search for solutions, the decision-maker tends to eliminate, to simplify. Poorly defined "soft" knowledge is displaced by quantitative information that appears to be more precise. Yet the policy errors of Vietnam suggest that soft is no less important than hard-nosed knowledge.[9]

This orientation — which is not wholly wrong, but not wholly right either — has two important sources in the social myths and values of the modern world. The first is the belief that "science" is primarily oriented toward, if not actually equal to, "human progress." The second important source is the "economizing" or "bookkeeping" approach associated with the increasing scale of business in the Western world since the seventeenth century. As scientific values have allied with business values as the basis for making social decisions, there has been a major shift in the patterns of myths and values to which the "elite" adhere.

The political character of modern resource decisions has been aggravated rather than diminished by the role of science. As the basis for public action science is not merely an intellectual process. It is an alliance of men with great technical knowledge and men with great economic and political power. Science contains its own internal processes of coercion and power.[10] And the technical knowledge that those processes of coercion and power defend is closely allied to the interests of existing economic and political elites.[11]

Thus , the problems of nuclear energy — discussed later in the chapter on "Faustian bargains" — were not produced by decisions of the ignorant. Rather, they were produced by the decisions of the most informed scientists, sustained by the highest military and political leadership during World War II, by the diplomatic and military leadership after the war, and by all of these plus the leadership of the electric power industry in the years after 1960.[12]

In a large-scale society, myths and values are never held unanimously. There are exceptions within any group, and there are always variations from one group to another. For example, social myths and values adhered to by U.S. factory workers and those adhered to by trained intellectuals in the United States differ substantially. In fact, one may hazard that trained intellectuals would more likely feel uncomfortable about accepting this very statement than would factory workers, to whom it would probably seem obvious. Evidence for these differences could be drawn from a number of sources, but two obvious indicators are public opinion data and actual social behavior. Public opinion polls — in the manner of Louis Harris, George Gallup, and others — suggest that exposure to formal education is a major divide between different schools of thought on civil liberties, race relations, party politics, and other controversial issues. A study of behavioral data, such as participation in antiwar activities before 1969 and financial support of environmental groups, would suggest a similar divide.

The close relationship of formal education to social attitudes is not surprising since it is one function of education to shape social myths and values. This is why people are concerned about who controls the schools and why education in a democratic polity has certain peculiar difficulties. Since the schools must have a certain degree of political support, they must not challenge too obviously the popular values. Yet mass education is also a system of transition in the sense that it trains people in social myths and values that equip them for a more elite status than that at which many of them began.

The major point is that even within a single population there is substantial variation in the myths and values that are held. The variations are more pronounced from one region of the world to another. Only if one is aware of these differences is it possible to explain the diverse responses of various Asian, African, and Latin American societies to the pressures of white expansion from the fifteenth century onward. In some cases, the pre-colonization societies virtually collapsed. Others, such as the Nez Perce and the Zulu, resisted militarily until their peoples were virtually exhausted by the greater military technology of the whites. Some states such as Ethiopia, when exposed to new cultures and changing ways, withdrew into a technological archaism and tenaciously maintained their old political class structures. Others such as China underwent something close to complete transformation — being torn apart by the pressures of the modern world — and only now are being reconstituted. Still others, such as Japan before World War II, were able to make rapid economic and technological adaptations, to largely preserve the essentials of their culture intact, and to grow in power beyond anything previously contemplated.[13]

These cultural differences have implications for natural resources issues. Presumably, most people — wherever they are — prefer eating to starving. In this light it was suggested some seven or eight years ago that, from the point of view of welfare economics,[14] the food supply of the Indian population could be improved if the various Indian state laws forbidding cattle slaughter were repealed.[15] Let us assume that, in terms of sheer caloric intake, the Indian people would be better off if they ate beef, rather than going completely meatless. Let us also assume that if beef were slaughtered, the local soil and vegetation would benefit from the reduced grazing. These assumptions alone would not make a repeal of cattle slaughter laws entirely rational. Most Indians are not welfare economists with a set of values derived from nineteenth century utilitarianism. Instead, they are devout followers of a religious tradition that opposes meat-eating not only for its members, but also for others. For that reason, the politics of repealing such legislation are extremely volatile, making a cattle slaughter plan as unthinkable as if there were no grass to feed the cattle or no trains to ship the meat. Even if options for policy change were not limited by the Indians' myths and values, they might be constrained by more practical matters for which the myths, in fact, may be a protection. That is, the slaughter of cattle might greatly reduce a critical source of fuel in India — cow dung.

Or, the repeal of the laws without the simultaneous creation of a cattle industry could result in the slaughter and consumption of all the cattle in India within a few weeks with no measurable effect on national nutrition.

This example should not be interpreted to mean that only those changes which are compatible with the prevailing pattern of myths and values should be proposed or attempted. For one thing, there is often such ambiguity about the pattern that it is difficult to tell in advance what is compatible and what is not. Even the proposal of apparently compatible changes may produce conflicts. More important, conflict itself is part of the adaptive process by which new ways of living are discovered. Patterns of social myths and values are always changing. Thus, conflict over myths and values is an important step in the persuasion of people who are changing their minds, or who are worrying over some problem they cannot solve unless they do change their minds.

The adoption of birth control practices by an increasing proportion of U.S. citizens represents something of this change process. Although advocacy of birth control can still produce, in some parts of the nation, political controversy of the bitter and rancorous sort that divides towns,[16] the situation is changing. Political figures with an eye to their constituencies (especially in Roman Catholic areas) who previously were either opposed or silent,[17] may now speak out favorably. Twenty years ago, one would have been hard put to find someone to predict that a conservative Supreme Court would uphold a qualified right to abortion,[18] that a state like New York (with an important Roman Catholic population) would adopt a statute to facilitate abortion, or that there would be substantial evidence that Roman Catholic women were simply ignoring the Church authorities in their personal practices.[19]

It is clear that solutions to the problems that people face are dictated by more than biological or physical realities. Social myths and values are ever present factors, affecting both the options that people perceive in their biological or physical environment and the ways in which they will interpret and act upon those options. Patterns of social myths and values are not unbreakable chains. But they do pose important constraints on all decision-making, including decisions on natural resources.

Institutions

Working within, and sometimes regardless of, the biophysical and cultural constraints of a society are the various institutions which make decisions and act upon options. The term *institution* may mean any one of three things: (a) a specific rule or practice, such as the interest rate set on a government loan; (b) a general pattern of action, such as the institution of monogamous marriage or the institution of private property; or (c) a specific organization with some charter, mission, or scope of authority. Whichever meaning one gives the word, the institution is something "infused with value" for the participants associated with it.[20]

Institutions and the decision-making processes associated with them constitute a somewhat independent system. The institution is not infinitely malleable nor is it necessarily responsive to the wishes of those who would change it. The independence of institutions is frequently suggested by students of Soviet agriculture as a source of that country's difficulty in meeting even the minimal food needs of its population.

"There are reasons," says Harry Rositzke, "for the poor agricultural performance of the USSR — not enough fertile land or rainfall, lack of tractor, combines, trucks, and fertilizers, repeated periods of bad weather. Between 1959 and 1967 there were only two good harvests (1964 and 1966) and the drought in 1963 was the worst in this century."[21] "Yet," Rositzke continues, "the basic fault lies in the [institutional] system itself."[22] The collective farms do not allow the peasant-producer enough incentive to put in his maximum effort. Crops are planned from decision levels too high up, too far away from the site to know exactly what will grow and what will not, and so forth.[23] Arcadius Kahan, an American economist, offers very specific illustrations of what he considers to be the failing in Soviet agricultural organization:

> Because the [central] planners could coerce the farms into following commands, errors were inflated to a very large scale. The list of such monumental blunders is very long indeed. It will suffice to mention the planting of rubber-yielding kok-saghyz, the planting of cotton on unirrigated lands in European Russia and the Ukraine, the expansion of corn to the north, or the plowing up of summer fallow in the east, as examples of the magnitude of damage inflicted by the planners and decision-makers.[24]

Kahan indicates other failures which grew out of mass indoctrination campaigns

> to which either all farms or a large number were inappropriately subjected. Such campaigns included a shelter-belt planting system, the attempts of universal introduction of the grassland system, the indiscriminate conversion of meadows into plowland, and the like.[25]

But, from another point of view, the system is not irrational. Its organization is based on past decisions about the values with which Soviet society should be infused. When the large-scale collectivization program was begun in 1928, a major objective was to break up the last remnants of private property and to impose a form of organization similar to that of industry. Thus, not only are the state farms and collective farms fixed features of Soviet agricultural organization, but even proposals to create smaller decision units called "links" within the collective farms are quite controversial and have, for the time being at least, been rejected. Laird, another student of Soviet agriculture, explains this by saying that

> Soviet leaders have shown themselves to be quite pragmatic at times. However, Soviet history also has demonstrated that political (and we believe ideological) motivations often are satisfied at considerable economic cost. Surely, the same political considerations that have been responsible for the stagnation of the Liberman reforms in industry also block a move to genuine economic accountability on the farms (and especially on the part of the individual peasant). Ideologically and politically, the prices paid for United States' grain and for tightened belts must not

seem as great as the losses which would result from genuinely relaxed central controls, particularly since the leaders must believe that enough new investments in the land will provide the ultimate solution.[26]

These observers (Rositzke, Kahan, and Laird) seem to say that the institutional system has much agricultural failure built into it.

The Soviet agricultural example is but one of an infinite series that one might have chosen. But it makes the central point. In thinking about natural resources, we have to think about both the specific institutions that govern natural resources decisions and the broader institutional context in which specific natural resources institutions are placed. Thus, Soviet agricultural policy would be incomprehensible if one looked only at agricultural organization, that is, the array of state farms, collective farms, and private plots. One has to keep in mind the essential requirements of the Soviet Union as a socialist society. One should also remember that those policy requirements that might appear marginal to the goal of a socialist society may be essential for the maintenance of government control. Precisely the same kind of point could be made about the organization of natural resources institutions in the United States or elsewhere.

References

1.   Peter Passell and Leonard Ross, *The Retreat from Riches: Affluence and Its Enemies* (New York: Viking, 1973), pp. 13-15.

2.   J. Willard Hurst, *Law and the Conditions of Freedom in the Nineteenth Century United States* (Madison: University of Wisconsin Press, 1967), pp. 3-6.

3.   For evidence to the point from at least thirteenth-century Italy to the nineteenth-century United States, see the chapter on "Administrative Law" in Alfred G. Donaldson, *Some Comparative Aspects of Irish Law* (Durham, N.C.: Duke University Press, 1957); John U. Nef, *Industry and Government in France and England, 1540-1640* (Ithaca, N.Y.: Cornell University Press, 1964), pp. 121-48.

4.   John R. Bunting, *The Hidden Face of Free Enterprise: The Strange Economics of the American Businessman* (New York: McGraw Hill, 1964), pp. 28-55.

5.   The classic work is Montesquieu, *The Spirit of the Laws*, translated by Thomas Nugent (New York: Hafner, 1949).

6.   Ellsworth Huntington, *Civilization and Climate* (New Haven: Yale University Press, 1915); *The Character of Races as Influenced by Physical Environment, Natural Selection and Historical Development* (New York: Scribner's, 1924).

7.   Whether this statement is true of the ruling elites of the rest of the world may be more doubtful. For example, it appears that many influential decision-makers in Sri Lanka consult astrologers as part of the normal process of coming to practical conclusions. Similar decision procedures outside the normal realm of secular science may be found in many other countries. And if the late William L. MacKenzie King could consult a spiritual medium or the late Bishop Pike could conceive of having the ability to communicate beyond the grave, it is possible that we overestimate the extent to which purely secular knowledge is accepted even in advanced industrial society.

8. For useful comment on the improper use of quantification see Harry Hopkins, *The Numbers Game: The Bland Totalitarianism* (Boston: Little, Brown, 1973), pp. 6-16; 33-46.

9. Guy Benveniste, *The Politics of Expertise* (Berkeley, Cal.: Glendessary Press, 1972), p. 55.

10. See discussion on "The consensual nature of research," Chapter 5, pp. 94-130 in Marlan Blissett's *Politics in Science* (Boston: Little, Brown, 1972).

11. Daniel S. Greenberg, *The Politics of Pure Science* (New York: New American Library, 1967), pp. 8-23; 270-76.

12. John M. Vernon, *Public Investment Planning in Civilian Nuclear Power* (Durham, N.C.: Duke University Press, 1971), pp. 125-30; 150-57. Also, H. Peter Metzger, *The Atomic Establishment* (New York: Simon and Schuster, 1972), pp. 234-37 and 245-49; Philip Mullenbach, *Civilian Nuclear Power* (New York: Twentieth Century Fund, 1963), pp. 97-111; 147-86.

13. Indeed, the puzzlement over the Japanese case was so great that in World War II the United States Government actually commissioned an anthropological analysis of the Japanese. See Ruth Benedict, *The Chrysanthemum and the Sword: Patterns of Japanese Culture* (Boston: Houghton Mifflin, 1946). David E. Apter, *The Political Kingdom in Uganda; A Study in Bureaucratic Nationalism* (Princeton, N.J.: Princeton University Press, 1961) makes a case that Uganda was also a highly adaptive and resistant society.

14. The seminal book is A. C. Pigou, *The Economics of Welfare* (London: Macmillan, 1952).

15. S. M. Mishra, "Cattle Meat and Economic Welfare," *Kylos* 19:1 (1966), pp. 119-22.

16. Kenneth W. Underwood, *Protestant and Catholic: Religious and Social Interaction in an Industrial Community* (Boston: Beacon Press, 1957), pp. 3-38.

17. John H. Fenton, *The Catholic Vote* (New Orleans: Hauser Press, 1960), pp. 7-20.

18. *Roe* v. *Wade*, 410 U.S 113, 93 S.Ct. 705, 35 L.Ed.2d 147 (1973); *Doe* v. *Bolton*, 410 U.S. 179, 93 S.Ct. 739, 35 L.Ed 2d 201 (1972).

19. Leslie A. Westoff and Charles F. Westoff, *From Now to Zero* (Boston: Little, Brown, 1968), pp. 163-206.

20. Philip Selznick, *Leadership in Administration* (New York: Harper & Row, 1957), pp. 17-20.

21. Harry Rositzke, *The USSR Today* (New York: John Day, 1973), pp. 44-45.

22. Ibid., p. 45. This view has also been expressed in Roy D. Laird and Betty A. Laird, *Soviet Communism and Agrarian Revolution* (Baltimore: Penguin, 1970), and by Arcadius Kahan, cited in notes 24 and 25 below.

23. Rositzke, *USSR Today*, p. 45.

24. Arcadius Kahan, "Agriculture," in Allen Kassof, ed., *Prospects for Soviet Society* (New York: Praeger, 1968), pp. 268-69.

25. Ibid., p. 269.

26. Roy D. Laird, "Politics and Soviet Agriculture in the 1970's: *Zerno* and the *Zveno*," paper presented to a meeting of the American Association for the Advancement of Slavic Studies, April 1973, pp. 15-16.

3. Estimates, Projections, and Forecasts

Predictions about the future — called forecasts — constitute the language of policy debate, the frames of reference that decision-makers take for themselves, and the bases of assumptions about what is or is not inevitable. How much wheat can the United States produce in the next three years? How much copper will be extracted over the next decade? When will demand for electricity exceed supply or vice versa? These are the kinds of questions that a forecast attempts to answer. Forecasts are vital tools for business and political leaders for they enable one to peer into the murky future and make reasonable predictions of when and where resource shortages may occur and what alternative sources of supply are available.

A forecast is a human judgment based on projections or other calculations. A projection is simply a mathematical device that extrapolates into the future a progression which has appeared as a trend in the past. Usually a given period in the past is taken for a baseline and the future time horizon is of equal or less duration than the baseline.

Forecasting, which often draws heavily on the quantification of mathematics,[1] should be viewed with an open and critical mind. This is not to minimize the value of forecasts. An educated guess as to the course of the future is far better than no guess at all. But it must be remembered that a forecast is just that — an educated guess, not a statement of fact. A forecaster's judgment is always subject to question, and sometimes his projections are too. This is particularly true when projections are based on estimates of resources that are "hidden" from man — dispersed through hundreds of miles of ocean or buried beneath 3,000 feet of earth — and whose true magnitude is difficult to know.

This chapter will show how estimates, projections, and forecasts are made, how they are used, and where their strengths and weaknesses lie.

Estimates

An estimate of supplies on hand is the first step in forecasting. Since early in this century both government and industry have sponsored resource estimates which are the backbone of market forecasts and government policies.

V. E. McKelvey describes the close link between resource estimates and resource policy:

> Faced with a developing shortage of natural gas, the Federal Power Commission is presently much interested in knowing whether or not reserves reported by industry are an accurate indication of the amount of natural gas on hand; it also wants to know the extent of potential resources and the effect of price on their exploration and development.[2]

Estimates of reserves influence decisions in many sectors of the economy. Estimates of oil, gas, and coal reserves influence government decisions on exploration subsidies, depletion allowances on natural gas, interstate natural gas prices, agency regulations on sulfur dioxide, research and development funding for new fuel supplies, and other questions. Similarly, a copper company will use information on ore reserves, market trends, and available technology in deciding how rapidly to develop existing mines, whether or not to open up new mines, and what kind of extraction or processing technology to order for the future.

How a resource is estimated depends upon the type of resource, whether it is living or nonliving, or, stated differently, whether it is renewable or nonrenewable.

While nonliving resources like minerals and fossil fuels may be continually undergoing concentration in minable quantities over a geological time span of millions of years, for man's practical purposes they are nonrenewable.

Biological resources, however, are regularly renewed, some of them every year when a new crop springs up or a new litter is born. The lifetime of the wheat plant or the tuna becomes the critical unit of time in the cycle of renewability. Yet even these self-sustaining resources can be seriously depleted for long periods of time by the mismanagement of an ecosystem or excessive exploitation of specific species. Moreover, once a species of plant or animal is exploited to extinction, its peculiar uniqueness can *never* be replaced, though other species may adapt to fill its function in the ecosystem.

Nonrenewable Resources: Distribution

The nonrenewable resources in which man has greatest interest are those useful to the human enterprise — metals, building materials, and fuels. However, minable concentrations of these mineral resources are both limited in number and irregularly distributed in space. Most rocks do not contain ore deposits. Only by geological accident and over millions of years of geological time were minerals deposited and concentrated in rock formations at a grade worth mining. Minerals occur rarely as a pure element and more commonly in association with other minerals as ores of varying grade. In addition all minerals exist in characteristic trace amounts known as crustal abundance. This is the average concentration of a mineral in the common rocks in a region where the mineral is not concentrated enough to be considered a deposit.

Iron, a very common mineral, may have a crustal abundance as high as 4.7 percent in shale and 6.8 percent in basalt.[3] Mercury, on the other hand, presently mined at an average 0.24 percent ore,[4] has a crustal abundance of 0.000,4 percent at the most.[5]

Though their minable deposits may occur only sporadically, specific minerals are characteristically associated with specific geological formations. For example, the majority of the U.S. coal beds were formed over 300 million years ago during the Pennsylvanian age and occur within sedimentary strata. Likewise, chromium deposits are commonly found in conjunction with rocks high in magnesium and nickel content.[6]

The size and richness of a mineral deposit, and whether the deposit is strictly localized or is dispersed at varying grades throughout a region, also depends on the type of mineral and its history of geological deposition. For example, lateritic nickel ore deposits often show a gradual enrichment from edge to center.[7] By contrast, a porphyry copper ore formed by repeated fracturing and mineralization may drop sharply from a high grade to a lower grade ore at the borders of the deposit. However, within the area of low grade ore, there may be pockets enriched by weathering.[8] Again, lead that has been deposited in limestone bedrock by mineral replacement will be concentrated in distinct veins. Immediately beyond the veins, lead will occur only in its crustal abundance.[9]

Petroleum and natural gas also demonstrate the sporadic distribution of mineral resources. Of the known oil and gas fields, 5 percent (238 fields) hold more than 85 percent of the world's production; 1 percent (55 fields) hold more than 65 percent, and two fields (Ghwar in Saudi Arabia and Burgan in Kuwait) hold more than 15 percent.[10]

In sea water, minerals are fairly evenly distributed but are highly diluted. Except for bromine, magnesium, sodium chloride, and a few other "minable" minerals, the sea's minerals are measured in ounces per million gallons.[11] It has been proposed that, with proper technology, minerals could be extracted from both sea water and the common rock of the earth's crust. However, the tremendous cost energy consumption and environmental degradation entailed in extracting trace minerals from either source would, at present, far outweigh the value of the mineral recovered.

Nonrenewable Resources: Estimates of Quantity

Making accurate estimates of mineral reserves for the future is currently impossible. Not only do minable mineral deposits occur irregularly, they also are frequently hidden from man's view by great depths of soil or common rock. This makes the search for new deposits a matter of educated guesswork and luck.

S. G. Lasky in 1950 attempted to estimate ore reserves of copper with a formula which showed that the tonnage of ore mined increased geometrically as the average grade to be mined decreased arithmetically.[12] Lasky based his theory on data from eight major porphyry copper deposits. And, as he himself pointed out, his method is valid only if the particular deposit in question actually occurs in a gradation from relatively rich to relatively lean material. While this relationship is true for some individual deposits, it is not true for ore deposits in general. High grade deposits are often abruptly isolated from the surrounding common rock. Aluminum and iron may be the only minerals to which Lasky's ratio may actually apply as a general rule.

Mineral search is guided mainly by past exploration and the knowledge that certain geological formations are favorable to the presence of a desired mineral. According to geologists Leet and Judson, "modern methods are best suited to extending old ore deposit outlines, or looking for new deposits under geological conditions similar to those where old ones were formed."[13] An example is a rock formation off Cape Hatteras that geologists suspect may be rich in oil because of its similarities to a formation underlying one of the great Arabian oil fields.[14]

Because of man's imprecise knowledge of mineral deposits, all estimates of reserves must begin with a count of those deposits which have been surveyed and are being economically mined with current technology. These are known as *proven reserves*.

Added to the proven reserves are those deposits which are known, have been roughly estimated, and could be mined with present or improved technology. However, these *ultimate recoverable reserves* are not necessarily currently economical nor have they been surveyed.

Recently the U.S. Geological Survey has adopted a new classification which distinguishes resource reserves by (1) feasibility of economic recovery and (2) degree of certainty of the deposit's existence.[15] In this classification, *identified resources* are specific bodies of mineral-bearing rock whose existence and location are known. These bodies are further divided into (1) *reserves*, identified resources which can be recovered at a profit with present technology and prices, and (2) *conditional resources* (or subeconomic resources), which must await higher prices or new technology to be economically recoverable.

The USGS describes undiscovered resources as either *hypothetical* or *speculative*. Hypothetical resources can reasonably be expected to occur in known districts or geological formations where deposits have occurred in the past. Speculative resources are suspected but as yet undiscovered deposits located in wholly unknown districts. Undiscovered resources are categorized only by the degree of certainty of their existence, not by economic factors.

Where mineral resources are in any of the "guess" categories, estimates are largely influenced by the estimator's opinion as to the feasibility and cost of extraction. For example, four separate estimates of current coal supplies in the United States started with a total of 32 billion tons in the ground, but each subdivided the total according to different assumptions and terminology.

As Figure 3.1 shows, the USGS in *Mineral Resources*, in keeping with their new terminology, divided the total coal tonnage into categories of *identified* and *hypothetical*, each equal to about 16 billion tons.[16] Since all coal districts are considered by USGS to be known, there is no *speculative* category for coal.

Identified 16 billion tons   (existence and location known)
Hypothetical 16 billion tons   (unidentified; expected to occur in known districts)

U.S. Mineral Resources,

pp. 137-38.

Identified — 16 billion tons

2 billion tons (a)
2 billion tons (b)
Conditional 12 billion tons (not currently recoverable)

Hypothetical 16 billion tons

(a) Recoverable, realistic estimate.

(b) Additional recoverable, liberal
       estimate.

Energy Resources of the U.S.,   p. 3.

Ultimately Recoverable Resources — 16 billion tons

Proved Recoverable Reserves 4 billion tons
Nonrecoverable 16 billion tons

Bituminous Coal Facts, 1972,   p. 9.

Minable — 16 billion tons

Mapped 8 billion tons
Unmapped 8 billion tons
Not Minable 16 billion tons

"Energy Resources," *Resources and Man,*

pp. 202-03.

3.1.   Four Different Estimates of United States Coal Resources.

Another USGS publication, *Energy Resources of the United States*,[17] elaborated on the *Mineral Resources* figures and further divided the *identified* 16 billion tons into two categories of *recoverable resources*, each based on a somewhat different assumption of economic recoverability, and a third category of *conditional* (or submarginal) *resources* that are not now recoverable.

A third estimate, published by the National Coal Association in *Bituminous Coal Facts, 1972*,[18] equated *proved recoverable reserves* with the more liberal of the two USGS figures for *identified recoverable reserves*, 4 billion tons, utilizing similar assumptions of current economic recoverability. However, while the 16 million tons of *ultimately recoverable reserves* reported in *Coal Facts* also matched USGS's tonnage of *identified resources*, these two figures were calculated from totally different assumptions. *Coal Facts* assumed that all 32 billion tons would be recoverable at a 50 percent rate while USGS postulated that 50 percent of all the coal in the ground had been identified.

M. King Hubbert combined both of these assumptions in his chapter on "Energy Resources" in the book *Resources and Man*.[19] He made the assumption of 50 percent technological recoverability to give 16 billion tons of minable coal. He then subdivided minable coal into *mapped* and *unmapped*, where mapped was synonymous with the USGS term *identified*. By using *recoverable* and *identified* coal as two independent assumptions each of which yielded 50 percent of the total coals, *minable mapped* coal thus became 50 percent of 50 percent, or 25 percent, of 32 billion tons.

The facts are known and the calculations are consistent in these four estimates of coal resources. But only if one is aware of the assumptions behind each estimate can he distinguish the pathways to the various subcategories. To make a sound decision on coal policy — or any other resource policy — one must know the assumptions underlying various estimates and be able to compare them.

Some minerals can be estimated more precisely than others because (1) their deposits are easy to find, (2) their deposits are characteristically large, and/or (3) exploration has been intensive.

No mineral in the United States has been explored as thoroughly as coal. Since all coal districts are now known, USGS has been able to subdivide its round figure of *proven reserves* into categories of *measured* (0.8 percent), *indicated* (26.8 percent), and *inferred* (65.2 percent) reserves.[20] The most imprecise category, *inferred*, means that the total amount of resource is known but its location may differ slightly from that given by the estimator. Coal is further classified by rank, thickness of seam, and nature of overburden.

While oil and gas reserves tend to occur in extensive fields, their fluid nature causes them to be mobile, continually seeking areas of lower pressure, moving from deeper, fine-grained rocks to shallower, porous rocks and always following the course of least resistance. This factor alone makes estimates of oil and gas in place difficult. But when oil and gas estimates are based on the *ultimately producible* amount, the chances for error become even greater.[21] These estimates draw not only on data of proven reserves, but also on past rates of production. This excludes allowances for new technology or for the vagaries of politics and economics, factors continually affecting man's resource exploitation.

Estimates of hardrock minerals are largely guesswork, as explained above. The USGS estimates the *identified resources* of U.S. copper at 76 million short tons, *hypothetical resources* at another 100 million short tons, and *speculative resources* at 120 million short tons.[22] There are also 111 million short tons of *conditional* copper resources which could become economically or technologically minable reserves at some future time.[23]

Renewable Resources: Estimating Wild Population

The picture is very different for estimates of renewable resources. Unlike mineral deposits whose distribution was determined by geological action many millions of years ago, the distribution of renewable resources is determined by environmental events of the present and the recent past and by man's cultivation and domestication.

The natural occurrence of wild species is highly correlated with climate and topography. Caribou, for example, are found between 45 degrees north latitude and the Arctic.[24] White pine prefer the sandy soils of the cool humid northeastern states and Canada.[25] However, within their range, many animal species move with the seasons, migrating from mountain tops to valleys or following the ocean currents. Over longer periods of time, plant species as well as animal species may be displaced from a particular location by competing species. For example, over a thirty-to-forty year period, large stands of aspen may disappear almost completely from a northern forest as they are shaded out by maples and pines.[26]

Density of organisms varies also. Some species congregate in herds, flocks, or pure timber stands while others are spaced far apart like the mink or the mahogany tree. To a degree, population size fluctuates from year to year depending on the severity of climate, food supply, disease, and predation (including that by man.)

Because of this variability in occurrence, wild populations that are commercially exploited must be estimated regularly. The total number of a species available for harvest or capture can be calculated from the age, sex, size, physiology, and behavior of individuals sighted or caught. Some estimates are surprisingly accurate. For example, a fact-finding committee of the International Whaling Commission reported that blue, humpback, and finback whale populations were so low that even with unrestricted whaling in 1963-1964, the industry would not be able to catch more than 8,500 blue whale units that year. Indeed, the industry caught only 8,429 units.[27]

However, despite the notable success of the whale commissioner's committee, estimates of wild populations are often unreliable simply because they depend on indirect measures. A case in point is the calculation devised by Pequegnat for estimating the annual krill population in Antarctic waters.[28] Krill, a shrimp-like creature *(Euphausia superba)*, is the main food of whales. Pequegnat estimated that an adult blue whale weighing approximately 90 tons swims an average speed of 4 knots with an energy exertion of 10 horsepower. Since the whale's muscles are only about 20 percent efficient in converting food to power, the blue whale needs 780,000 calories per day for propulsion. Adding other caloric requirements which are estimated from the whale's surface area, it follows that the animal needs over 1 million calories a day. If krill delivers 460 calories per pound, a swimming blue whale requires 2,200 pounds of krill. A *growing* whale needs another 600 to 800 pounds a day or roughly a ton and a half of krill. Since the whales feed only six months per year the figure is doubled to 3 tons per day. Using the 1910 population estimate of Antarctic whales of half a million, Pequegnat calculated that, at 3 tons of krill per day for six months, krill consumption by whales would amount to 270 million tons per year. Whales however at best catch only 20 percent of the available krill, making the total annual krill production 1,350 million tons. Since krill feeding pastures cover about 3.5 million square miles, this averaged about 1,000 pounds of krill per acre.

More recent estimates put the total biomass of krill as high as 10 billion gross tons, almost eight times more than Pequegnat's figure.[29] While no completely reliable estimate of krill is yet available, current methods of calculation based on sampling data (measures of krill density and total population dispersion over time)[30] are more direct and, for this reason, more credible.

Estimating wild plant populations is usually easier than measuring animals. Trees, obviously, occupy the same place for long periods of time. In temperate deciduous or conifer forests which have only a handful of dominant species, the reserve of standing trees can be calculated very precisely by sample counting of timber stands. But in virgin or semivirgin tropical rain forests characterized by a high number of different species, all closely intermingled, calculations can be difficult. In such a forest there may be less than one harvestable individual of a particular species per hectare (2.47 acres) on an average, and the same hectare may contain up to 100 or more different species. With the development of aerial photography, valuable but widely dispersed timber trees such as mahoganies and teaks now can be spotted from the air and then pinpointed by a grid survey on the ground.[31]

Renewable Resources: Estimating Domesticated Populations

Within his highly managed agricultural systems, man can direct the basics of biological growth — water, air, and nutrients — to produce a variety of end products. There are regional limitations to this variety, of course, set by day length, temperature, rainfall, and soil. But within these limits, land can be used for all manner of produce. The fact that the North American land area amounts to 5.21 billion acres, of which 1.14 billion acres are arable and of which 590 million acres were under cultivation in 1969, roughly indicates *potential* productivity only.[32] That land can be withdrawn at any time from the pool of cultivation by urban development or surface mining. Expanding one land use means sacrificing another; even expanding the acreage of a particular crop means either converting acreage normally used for another crop or withdrawing idle, and possibly marginal, land from the reserves. Therefore, it is not surprising that agricultural resources are not expressed as absolute estimates, but rather as figures that reflect the probable crop to be harvested in the current season.

For example, forecasts of the 1973 corn crop began in January of the year with U.S. Department of Agriculture surveys of planting intentions, that is, acres intended to be planted to corn; as follows: January, 70.5 million acres; March, 72 million acres; April, 74.1 million acres.

Knowing the yields of 1971 (rather low at 88.1 bushels per acre) and 1972 (high at 96.9 bushels per acre), one could foresee a range of possible yields. In July, with the crop in good growth, the USDA forecast that the 62.5 million acres actually planted would yield 94 bushels per acre, a total of 5.88 billion bushels. By August this forecast was revised to 5.66 billion, and in September, when harvest began, the number had firmed up at 5.768 billion bushels.[33]

In contrast to crop estimates, the forecasts of domesticated animal populations are established by censuses at given moments of time and the numbers are precise for the date of the census.

Two factors explain why crop and livestock forecasts are rarely extended beyond a single year: (1) reliable long-term climatic forecasts are not yet possible, and (2) the crop produced depends on the market. For example, the amount of livestock produced in a given season depends on the respective domestic and foreign markets for corn, wheat, soybeans, and feed grains as well as household budgets for red meat and poultry. Whether a corn crop becomes hog feed or corn meal depends on the market price for pounds of pork versus bushels of corn.

The Dynamics of Estimating

As we saw in the discussion of mineral resources, estimates are dynamic. With improved mining technology and greater geologic knowledge, estimates become more certain and tons of ore are moved from a speculative to a hypothetical status or from a conditional to a reserve status. (Figure 3.2 illustrates the rise in oil production which followed each innovation in prospecting technology.) In a similar way, with satellite tracking of large schools of fish, fish catch estimates become more accurate. Aerial surveys of tropical forests not only increase the reliability of timber estimates by also facilitate the harvest of valuable trees.

The economy, which itself is dynamic and cyclic, has a direct bearing on estimates. Table 3.1 shows how the 1968 estimates of recoverable copper reserves varied with the probable price per pound of refined copper.[34]

Just as the profitability of mineral exploitation is built into the concept of proven reserves, the proportion of acreage given to a particular crop is determined by the farm market. Fisheries, forestry, and fur trade also fluctuate with market prices.

Finally, changes in scientific theory may accelerate or slow down the discovery or development of resources, ultimately affecting the estimates. For example, in 1968, after forty-five years of dormancy, Alfred Wegener's (1880-1930) theory on

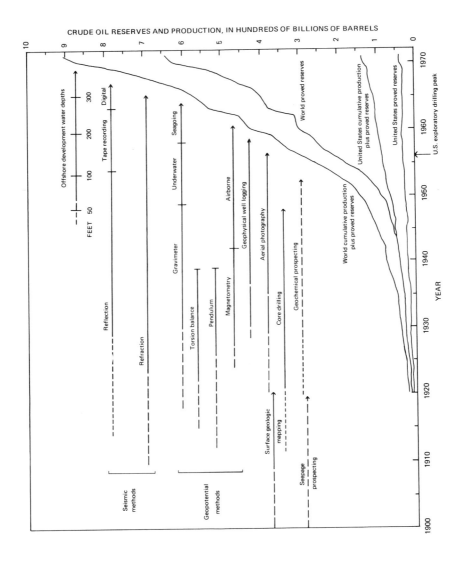

3.2.   Effects of Technological Innovation on the Rates of Discovery and Production of Crude Oil.

TABLE 3.1. Long-Run Copper Supply Response to Price

	Recoverable copper (million short tons)	
Price of copper (1968 dollars per pound)	United States	Foreign
$0.50	81	215
$0.60	94	238
$0.70	94	268
$0.80	99	303
$0.90	100	341
$1.00	135	381
$1.10	147	426
$1.20	159	478
$1.30	172	537
$1.40	185	606
$1.50	198	687

Source: "Copper Pricing Practices," Hearings before House Committee on Interstate and Foreign Commerce, July 1970, p. 20.

continental drift was revived in the United States in a modified form called plate tectonics.[35] By 1973, most USGS geologists had adopted the new position and were using it to explain the geographical distribution of orebodies as well as to predict the sites of possible new finds. As a case in point, mercury deposits are now thought to have been formed in subduction zones[36] on the edge of tectonic plates in post-Jurassic times.[37] The search for mercury presently is focused on areas within that geologic formation.[38] Thus new theory brings about a change in perspective. While the final proof of a mineral deposit is whether or not the hammer or drill hits paydirt, the mineral must be sought first in the geologist's mind.[39]

Biological theory also undergoes change which affects the exploitation of renewable resources for better or worse. For example, the low agricultural productivity of Stalinist Russia was partly due to the obsolete theories held by Trofim Lysenko, president of the Lenin Academy of Agricultural Sciences for twenty-five years. Lysenko, who became a kind of "biological Rasputin," combined Marxism and outdated Lamarckian thought into regressive theories on genetics and heredity which stunted Russian progress in plant and animal breeding for many years.[40]

Projections and Forecasts

An estimate of the resource supply on hand is only half the information needed to make resource decisions. One must also know what the future production potential and the future demand for that resource will be. Forecasts of future production and demand, like estimates of supply, involve much guesswork. But the guesses are based on very different kinds of information and methods of assembling data.[41]

The forecaster of future demand looks for statistical trends in the rates of resource use. One technique he commonly employs is the *trend projection*. This method assumes that the rate of change of a variable, such as electricity consumption, will continue unchanged in the future. Thus, the trend projected is simply an extrapolation of past rates of resource use.

According to economist P. A. Samuelson,[42] economists and statisticians base their projections on four sources: (1) statistics based on the GNP, personal income, new construction, equipment spending, and indices of price, production, or store sales; (2) polls, such as the McGraw-Hill questionnaire of business intentions; (3) models of consumption, investment, and government expenditures which assume that certain relationships between these three variables reflect the state of business fairly accurately;[43] (4) leading economic indicators of the past which are followed through time. To make a forecast the expert weighs the results of these methods and takes the most likely of a number of futures as his rule for action. It is in the weighing of the respective importances of *multiple projections* that a forecast differs from the single trend projection.

General vs. Specific Assumptions in Forecasting

Since forecasts involve judgments, they of necessity include assumptions. Some assumptions are so general that they are not worth stating — that is, the sun will shine and there will be people next year. Others, like major wars, enter the picture so irregularly that they also are not stated.

However, the specific assumptions which a forecaster uses in his extrapolations must be stated.[44] They are part of the detailed reasoning that went into the projections and are the basis for judgments made in the forecast. For example, many quantifiable assumptions are involved in a projection of residential electrical demand and should be stated in the resulting forecast: changing patterns of living (from single family homes to condominiums and apartments); the changing size and number of households; the changing patterns of family budgets as per capita buying power grows; the impact of inflation; and the impact of newly invented commodities or services. In addition, pertinent demographic data (birth rate, death rate, fertility rate, age structure, and the situation of the elderly) must be defined. Assumptions about weather are also crucial since air conditioning and space heating have made the utilities "weather-sensitive" all year round. However, in the absence of good long-range weather projections, the weather generally is assumed "normal" or constant.

Similarly, forecasts of electrical demand for the commercial, agricultural, and industrial sectors (including transportation, fabrication, and processing) should include concrete statements about the variables influencing the economy, particularly the economy of the resource being studied.

Time Assumptions in Forecasting

Forecasts usually are short-term, medium-run, or long-term. Specialists within an industry use these terms to express an important relationship between time and the forecast: a long-term forecast assumes that *all* costs, both capital and operating, are variable or uncertain: a short-term projection means that capital costs are known and only operating costs remain uncertain.

Thus, given the land and capital of a farmer and his intent to plant wheat, a short-term forecast can be made of his probable wheat production. This is done without certain knowledge of the final costs in time and labor, but, barring calamities, this kind of forecast can be fairly accurate.

However, a forecast of copper output twenty-five years hence is long-range, and by implication is a more uncertain estimate. Many of the factors that will effect future operating costs of mine and smelter are presently undetermined. Will there be labor strikes against producers between now and then? What limits will new labor contracts impose? Will there be substantial increases in rail freight rates? The capital costs are also only roughly estimated and could be greatly altered by inflation, rising land costs, the discovery of a copper substitute, the development of a new smelting technology, or the expanding operations of a competitor.

Because of such numerous uncertainties, all production forecasts should state where the latest decision — and the commitment it implies — stands with regard to the string of decisions that are necessary for final production of a commodity. For example, the formation of a subsidiary copper company to explore a promising deposit does not entail an irreversible commitment to open a new mine. To obtain a bank loan for mine construction does show serious intent and indicates a high likelihood that the new mine will be built. To let contracts for mine construction shows strong commitment to completing the project.

As mentioned earlier, forecasts of renewable resources are short-range — generally only a year ahead, sometimes up to five years. When they extend beyond that period, assumptions become so numerous and uncertain that the results can only be taken as speculation. A case in point is the FAO study, *Agricultural Commodity Projections 1970-1980.*[45] The study deals with the whole world, and its assumptions are formidable. They include population, income, agricultural policy, and international trade. Minimal change in crop growth patterns is assumed and the forecasts stay very close to projections. World population growth is assumed to be 2.6 percent compounded annually. A modest overall increase in crop tonnage is foreseen with highest rates of increase occurring in developing countries.

A major flaw in the FAO study is that it takes no account of climate change over the ten-year period. An accurate extended agricultural forecast would require that one know the future climate. This is something currently beyond our abilities. While it may be possible to forecast climatic trends over periods of hundreds of years, the yearly fluctuations which are more immediately critical are much less predictable. As recent events around the world have shown, unseasonable weather over a three- or four-year period can wreak havoc with populations which have already grown beyond their food resources.[46]

One fairly satisfactory way to handle the uncertainties of weather and changes in land use is to base crop production estimates on the spread between the lowest and highest crops of the last decade. The Canadian Wheat Board commonly bases its projections on this measure.[47]

As with crops, timber production can be projected to some extent, but major uncertainties remain regarding the actual cubic feet or wood added per year per acre and possible changes in the use of forest land. A ten-year projection for the U.S. timber crop may be more reliable than a similar long-term estimate for corn production, but it is certainly more risky than projecting minerals production ten years hence.

How Forecasts Are Used

All forecasts serve a purpose. In most cases, the purpose is to provide an objective answer to a question. In other cases, a forecast may be designed to serve as evidence in support of an individual's or an organization's wishes. This bias may manifest itself in the extrapolations or in the manner that data is presented. To avoid bias as much as possible, the variables underlying the forecast must be clarified and the time horizons must be linked organically to the phenomena they define. Forecasts should be stated in multiple answers and, if possible, probabilities should be attached to them, or a statistical range based upon standard errors.

Despite precautions, however, bias is almost unavoidable, since individual judgment is the deciding element in the compilation of a forecast. All too often the beneficiary himself makes the forecasts and lets his judgment be tainted by self-interest. And, if one has had long experience in a field, there is danger of falling into a comfortable routine of predicting the habitual and avoiding much thought about new factors that might alter the forecast. Even some major corporations, those institutions with perhaps the greatest access to new analytical techniques, can be seen, after the fact, to have been guided by their own optimism instead of by appraisals of new factors that were visible to their less hidebound counterparts.[48] Finally, many an executive weighs the possible effect of his forecasts on his career.

If bias is inevitable in forecasting, who is to be entrusted with making our national resource forecasts?

There are obvious reasons for not giving the task to a single agency of government such as a vast U.S. Census Bureau or a super U.S. Bureau of Mines. Such an agency would be subject to pressures from other branches of government and from private industry to produce "favorable" forecasts. Moreover it might well want to carve a place for itself as *the* agency for planning, with all the dangers that implies. It would have a monopoly over data, it would be the only oracle, and it could be subverted easily to the service of narrow interests.

One solution would be a plurality of independent competitive data banks. We would know much more about the energy crisis if several independent forecasting firms, holding data for all forms of energy, could be consulted. Ideally such organizations would include a whole spectrum of resource forecasts in order to avoid a vicious cycle of reliance on other firms' forecasts. For example, it would be preferable for firms A, B, and C each to make independent forecasts of coal, oil, and gas reserves rather than A having to rely on B's forecast of oil which was derived from C's calculations which drew upon A's figures on coal and gas.

Again, ideally, independent data banks should provide forecasts on request to any customer who consults them. But, at present, the last condition seems impossible. While several private consulting firms with their own data banks do now exist, the expenses of these firms are such that only major corporations can afford their services and the data center's interests are almost inevitably tied to its major customers.

Many of our predictions today emanate from national associations of producers or manufacturers, banks, and government agencies, all of which are clearly influenced to varying degrees by the constituencies they serve. Even a major policy forecast such as the 1970 National Power Survey of the Federal Power Commission can be criticized for being somewhat less than neutral. How the survey reached the conclusions it did on electrical energy demand can be partly understood by considering who made the forecast.

A Case Study: The National Power Survey

The 1970 National Power Survey was undertaken by the Federal Power Commission to provide forecasts from 1970 to 1990 for the electric utility industry.[49] The survey has exercised considerable influence on decision-making processes and its prediction of a ten-year doubling time for electric demand has been and continues to be used extensively. This prediction is the major message of the four-volume study and is consistent with what has actually occurred in the past three decades.

However, some of the methods used in preparing the report raise questions as to its purported status as a neutral document. The report's reviewing committee, consisting of one representative each from the Atomic Energy Commission, the Association of Illinois Electrical Cooperatives, and the Commonwealth Edison Company, was a mixed group but hardly a disinterested one.[50] Nor was there disinterest among the regional advisory committees, which were drawn primarily from the utility industry and approved each chapter of the report.[51]

Not only did the utilities provide the survey with raw data, as one would expect, but they also made their own forecasts. Each utility's forecast was based on projections for its own region and included anticipated results of promotional programs. Also included in the regional forecasts were results of surveys of consumer buying intentions and market saturation of appliances as well as predictions about the outcome and effects of the national electric power forecast. All the individual utility forecasts — in effect, numerous individual judgments — were added up to provide the national picture,[52] a process called "the Building Block Method" by the Battelle Memorial Institute's study of forecasts.[53]

In reality the judgments of each utility could be interpreted as business decisions more or less informed by projections. The individual forecasts that went into NPS 70 seemed to be the most favorable extrapolations of electric demand that the utilities dared to predict for their areas. Therefore the sum of these forecasts could not give a different picture: the future was as sanguine as the consensus of the utilities dared to envision.

Throughout the text of the survey only two of the forecasts are obviously based on multiple projections and offer to the reader a range of high, medium, and low estimates for any year in the future.[54]

A flat assumption is made in NPS 70 that the electrical demand of residential appliances is totally inelastic or independent of price.[55] From this follows an unstated but important assumption that saturation of the appliance market is an accurate measure of expected new demand. This assumption does not take into account that as prices go up, people may buy fewer electrical appliances or insist on more efficient appliances. Consequently, NPS 1970 forecasts major increases in all-electric homes despite rises in utility rates. Gas- or oil-heated homes are expected to be highly electrified by 1990 due to numerous appliances, air conditioners, and auxiliary electric space heaters.[56]

However, according to the econometric survey of Mount et al. sponsored by Oak Ridge National Laboratory and based on 1970 census data, utility prices are a major variable in electric demand of residential and other demand sectors.[57] The survey predicts that the NPS forecasts cannot materialize. While NPS 1970 forecasts a little under 5 to 6 billion megawatts/hr of electric power demand by 1990, the Oak Ridge study has a high forecast of 3 billion megawatts per hour while its medium and low projections are much less. For further discussion of the Oak Ridge model, see Chapter 4, pp. 46-50.

Finally, possible bias in NPS 1970 is suggested in its discussion of construction delays. A table[58] shows environmental litigation as the cause for twenty-five cases of construction delays on steam-electric generating plants between 1966 and 1970. During the same period, there were 155 labor-related delays and 104 delays due to equipment failure or late delivery. Yet the text emphasizes environmental delays, citing the controversy over the Storm King (Cornwall, New York) pump storage hydropower project on the Hudson River,[59] the *Calvert Cliffs* case,[60] and air and water quality standards.[61]

There seems to be no easy solution for removing bias from forecasts. Yet the more serious the problems of natural resources utilization become, the more pressing become the questions of how forecasts are drawn up and how predictions influence policy One method that seems to hold some promise for improving forecasts is modeling. The next chapter will discuss how models are being used to forecast energy demand and to broaden resource planners' views of the future.

References

1. The use of mathematical models as a tool in forecasting is discussed in Chapter 4.
2. V. E. McKelvey, "Mineral Resource Estimates and Policy," in D. A. Brobst and W. A. Pratt, eds., *United States Mineral Resources*, USGS Paper 820 (Washington, D.C.: U.S. Government Printing Office, 1973), pp. 10-11.
3. Thomas A. Lovering, "Mineral Resources from the Land," in Committee on Resources and Man, National Academy of Sciences - National Research Council, *Resources and Man* (San Francisco: Freeman, 1969), p. 11.
4. E. H. Bailey, A. L. Clark, and R. M. Smith, "Mercury," in Brobst and Pratt, *U.S. Mineral Resources*, pp. 404, 406.
5. Lovering, "Mineral Resources from the Land," *Resources and Man*, p. 111.

6. T. P. Thayer, "Chromium," in Brobst and Pratt, *U.S. Mineral Resources,* p. 112. Also, Paul Averitt, "Coal," ibid., p. 134.
7. Lovering, "Mineral Resources from the Land," *Resources and Man,* p. 116.
8. Ibid., p. 114.
9. Ibid., p. 115.
10. J. H. McCulloh, "Oil and Gas," in Brobst and Pratt, *U.S. Mineral Resources,* p. 481.
11. Preston Cloud, "Mineral Resources from the Sea," in *Resources and Man,* p. 140.
12. Lovering, "Mineral Resources from the Land," *Resources and Man,* pp. 112-14.
13. L. D. Leet, and S. Judson, *Physical Geography* (Englewood Cliffs, N.J.: Prentice-Hall, 1965), p. 346.
14. McCulloh, "Oil and Gas," *U.S. Mineral Resources,* p. 490.
15. Introduction, *U.S. Mineral Resources,* pp. 3-5.
16. Averitt, "Coal," *U.S. Mineral Resources,* pp. 136-40.
17. P. K. Theobald, S. P. Schweinfurth, and D. C. Duncan, *Energy Resources of the United States,* U.S. Geological Survey Bulletin 650 (Washington, D.C.: U.S. Government Printing Office, 1972), pp. 3-4.
18. *Bituminous Coal Facts, 1972,* National Coal Association, (Washington, D.C.: 1972), p. 9.
19. M. King Hubbert, "Energy Resources," in *Resources and Man,* pp. 201-04.
20. Averitt, "Coal," *U.S. Mineral Resources,* Figure 16, p. 138.
21. McKelvey, "Mineral Resource Estimates and Public Policy," *U.S. Mineral Resources,* p. 15.
22. D. P. Cox, R. G. Schmidt, J. D. Vine, H. Kirkemo, E. B. Tourtelo, and M. Fleischer, "Copper," in *U.S. Mineral Resources,* Table 39, p. 180; Table 40, p. 183. (A short ton is 2,000 pounds.)
23. Ibid., p. 184.
24. Randolph L. Peterson, *The Mammals of Eastern Canada* (Toronto: Oxford University Press, 1966), pp. 332-34.
25. *Silvics of Forest Trees of the U.S.,* Agricultural Handbook No. 271, Forest Service, U.S. Department of Agriculture, 1965, pp. 329-30.
26. John T. Curtis, *Vegetation of Wisconsin* (Madison: University of Wisconsin Press, 1959), p. 207.
27. Since the first whale species hunted was the large blue whale, all catch is calculated in blue whale units which correspond to the 90-ton "standard" adult blue whale. Thus, two finback, or two and a half humpback whales equal one blue whale unit: Scott McVay, "The Last of the Great Whales," *Scientific American,* August 1966, reprinted in J. R. Moore, ed., *Oceanography* (San Francisco: Freeman, 1970), p. 314.
28. W. E. Pequegnat, "Whales, Plankton, and Man," *Scientific American,* January 1958, reprinted in *Oceanography,* pp. 278-79.
29. George A. Llano, "Antarctica," *Encyclopaedia Britannica,* 12th ed., vol. 2, p. 8.
30. G. A. Knox, "Antarctic Marine Ecosystems," in M. W. Holgate, ed., *Antarctic Ecology* (New York: Academic Press, 1970), pp. 69-96; J. A. Gulland, "The Development of the Resources of the Antarctic Seas," *Antarctic Ecology,* pp. 217-23. For further discussion of methods to estimate aquatic populations, see for example *Introduction to the Fishery Sciences* (New York: Academic Press, 1972), pp. 226-31.
31. L. E. Eeckhout, *L'exploitation forestière au Congo Belge.* Ministère des Colonies (Brussels: 1953), pp. 20-24. See also P. W. Richards, *The Tropical Rain Forest* (Cambridge: Cambridge University Press, 1952).

32. Data from P. Ehrlich and A. Ehrlich, *Population, Resources, Environment: Issues in Human Ecology* (San Francisco: Freeman, 1970), p. 91.

33. *Farm Journal*, vol. 97 (1973) for the months February, April, May, August, September, October, respectively.

34. U.S., Congress, House, Committee on Interstate and Foreign Commerce, "Copper Pricing Practices," Hearings, 91st Congress, 2nd session, July 20-21, 1970, p. 20.

35. Marlan Blisset, *Politics in Science* (Boston: Little, Brown, 1972), pp. 131-32.

36. The edge of one plate may be pushed under the edge of another abutting plate. The superimposed edges are then called *subduction zones*.

37. Within the last 63 million years of geologic time.

38. E. H. Vailey, A. L. Clark, and R. M. Smith, "Mercury," in *U.S. Mineral Resources*, pp. 409-11.

39. W. E. Pratt, *Oil in the Earth* (Lawrence: Kansas University Press, 1942), p. 49.

40. C. D. Darlington, "The Retreat from Science in Soviet Russia," *Nineteenth Century*, 142: 164-65 (1948).

41. See M. Adelson, *The Technology of Forecasting and the Forecasting of Technology*, Systems Development Corporation (Santa Monica, Cal.: 1968).

42. P. A. Samuelson, *Economics: An Introductory Analysis*, 8th ed. (New York: McGraw-Hill, 1970), p. 248.

43. See Chapter 4 for discussion of modeling.

44. See Chapter 4, pp. 52-57, for an example of assumptions being stated when constructing a model for energy demand.

45. Food and Agricultural Organization, *Agricultural Commodity Projections 1970-1980*, U.N. Publication, (Rome: 1971).

46. Tom Alexander, "Ominous Changes in the World's Weather," *Fortune*, February 1974, p. 90.

47. Communication to Leonardo Seminar, May 2, 1973, by members of the Canadian Wheat Board.

48. Richard A. Smith, *Corporations in Crisis* (Garden City, N.Y.: Doubleday, 1963), pp. 157-69.

49. 1970 National Power Survey, Report by the Federal Power Commission, 4 vols. (Washington, D.C.: U.S. Government Printing Office, 1971).

50. Ibid., vol. I, p. 23.6.

51. Ibid., pp. 23.2-23.4; p. 3.12.

52. Ibid., p. 3.12.

53. *A Review and Comparison of Selected United States Energy Forecasts*, Battelle Memorial Institute (Columbus, Ohio: December 1969), pp. 9-10.

54. 1970 National Power Survey, vol. I, p. 1.34 (Table 1.8), p. 3.15, p. 3.17 (Figure 3.7). The advantages of projecting several alternate futures are discussed below in Chapter 4.

55. Ibid., vol. 1, pp. 3.4-3.5.

56. Ibid., vol. 1, p. 3.8.

57. T. Mount, D. Chapman, and T. Tyrell, *Electricity Demand in the United States: An Econometric Analysis*, Oak Ridge National Laboratory Report NSF-EP-49 (Oak Ridge, Tenn.: 1973). Econometrics is the application of statistical methods to the study of economic data and problems.

58. *1970 National Power Survey*, vol. 1, p. 16.3 (Table 16.2).

59. *Scenic Hudson Preservation Conference v. FPC*, 354 F. 2d 608, (2nd Cir. 1965).

60. *Calvert Cliffs Coordinating Committee v. AEC*, 449 F. 2d 1109, (D. C. Cir. 1971).

61. *1970 National Power Survey*, vol. I, pp. 16-6 to 7.

4. Models: Finding Alternative Futures

To see the future, particularly the "energy demand" future, more clearly, forecasters are turning increasingly to various types of models. Like other forecasting methods, models have their limitations. They are only as accurate or as objective as model-builders allow them to be. Yet some models have an advantage that other forecasting techniques•lack: they offer the opportunity to find an "optimal future" by experimenting in advance, on paper or on a computer, with the probable consequences of numerous different policies. Prudent use of these methods ultimately may enable us to invent the future we wish to live in rather than suffer the future that we would not or could not see.

This chapter will attempt to give some insight into what models are, how they are being applied to current energy problems, and what contributions they can make to resource management.

What is a Model?

For our purposes, a model is "a representation or abstraction of an actual object or situation."[1] It can be a physical representation like the model aircraft flown by engineers in a wind tunnel, or it can be an abstract mathematical model like the equations which the aeronautical engineer uses to describe the laws or theory governing flight. Whatever its form, a model does not appear naturally. It is made by man to serve a purpose, often to facilitate communication or instruction regarding complex subjects.

The purpose of an energy demand model generally is (1) to describe a *system*, that is, an aggregation of units or *variables* that are joined together in some regular interaction or interdependence, and (2) to show the relationships between these variables, including, if possible, causes and effects. Such a model also may be designed to point out those units which are the important ones for answering specific questions about the system.

Model-building always begins with a *theory* or *question,* an unproven idea or concept. An experiment of verification, which can take the form of a field test or some type of measurement, then may support the theory or answer the question. Or,

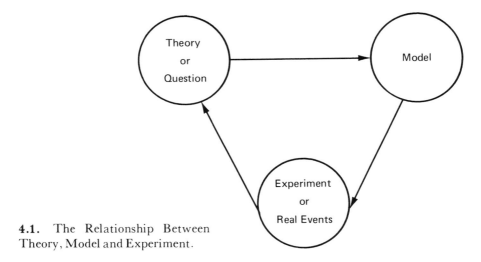

4.1. The Relationship Between Theory, Model and Experiment.

it may disprove the theory, thus requiring revision and further model-building. Figure 4.1 shows the circular path of relationships between theory, its model, and its verification by experiment or by the onward march of real events. This *feedback* loop is also the process by which man's knowledge grows.[2]

The cycling is a continuous process that rarely stops for long, since new knowledge evolves continuously. Time too affects the feedback system to the extent that hypothetical future events forecast by the model do or do not occur.

The feedback cycle shows that even if a model fails to predict change satisfactorily, that failure can help indicate flaws in the model or in the model-builder's concept of the system. Since all models must be tested in hindsight, failure can be a necessary step in the development of a sophisticated model.

There are three basic criteria for evaluating the performance of a model: *realism, precision,* and *generality.*[3] Realism describes how well the mathematical statements of the model correspond to the concepts or processes which they are meant to represent. Precision is the model's ability to predict numerical change. Generality refers to the breadth of applicability of the model — in other words, the number of different situations in which it can be used. Just which of these three objectives should have the highest priority in model-building depends upon the specific application.

Characteristics of Models

Much model-building begins on a theoretical basis and eventually evolves to the state at which it can be quantified. For example, a simplistic model often used in energy forecasts states that annual per capita energy usage is proportional to annual gross national product per capita (GNPPC) or, symbolically,

$$E = BG$$

where E = a variable representing annual energy usage per capita;

           G = a variable representing annual gross national product per capita;

and B = the constant of proportionality relating E and G.

If B is then given a statistical value, such as 60,000 BTU per dollar of GNP, the model takes on the *quantitative* form

$$E = 60,000 \cdot G,$$

allowing the modeler to calculate E if G is known or postulated.

Each model has its own relationship to time. A *static model* describes a fixed system that will not change significantly in the time span under consideration. However, in a *dynamic model,* the time factor plays a significant role in the sequence of events.

Finally, all models have some type of *hierarchical organization* of smaller components within bigger components. This organization helps the model-user decide how much detail he needs to know. It is not necessary to understand precisely how a system is structured from its simplest components in order to predict its behavior.[4] For example, the rising of a cake mix can be described without a complete

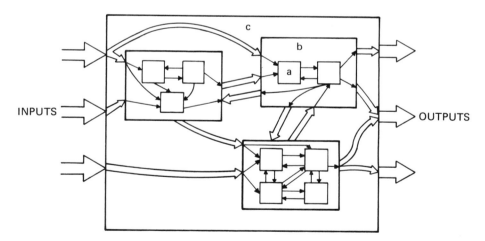

4.2.   The Hierarchical Organization of Systems. Letters a, b, and c represent three levels of organization or "black boxes" made up of simpler black boxes. By observing the input and output of box c, one can predict its behavior without having to understand its simpler components, a - b. Or, one can predict box b's behavior from its input and outputs without any knowledge of the simpler component a. *Source:* E. P. Odum, *Fundamentals of Ecology,* W. B. Saunders Company (1971)

knowledge of the chemistry of yeast. Similarly, when an industry's electricity demand changes in response to a new electricity price, the change can be described without reference to the details of the industrial process.

This hierarchical structure is illustrated in Figure 4.2, where the components of a system (often called "black boxes") are interconnected by linkages (arrows) representing the interactions between components. If the *input-output relationship* is known for a particular box, its behavior can be predicted *without* understanding how it is put together from simpler components.

Which level of subdivision (which level of boxes within boxes) does the modeler use? This depends on the purpose of the model. For general forecasting, gross representation of a system may be sufficient. For example, electric utility planners commonly extrapolate the trend of output from *only one* box, "total capacity," to get a forecast of future gross generating capacity. For this purpose, a more detailed breakdown of the various electricity demand components is unnecessary.

Trend Projections

Figure 4.3 shows the trend, based on the "total capacity" box, for all electric utilities in Wisconsin. This method is the familiar trend projection discussed in Chapter 3 (p. 34). It is one of the simplest and most commonly used models in energy demand forecasting. Although it is not necessarily more accurate than other methods, the trend projection has been well-suited to following the persistent and characteristic growth rates of U.S. energy consumption over the past several decades. For example, Figure 4.4 shows that a simple linear projection on a semilogarithmic scale would have provided good forecasts of Wisconsin electricity sales during the past two decades, since doubling time has remained almost constant at approximately 9.5 years.[5]

However, trend projection does not apply as well to natural gas consumption, which grew in spurts (Figure 4.5). Between 1955 and 1963, the doubling time for gas consumption was four years. Although the growth has slowed recently, throughout the later 1960s gas remained the fastest growing primary energy fuel in Wisconsin, with a doubling time of seven years. As a result of this sporadic growth, a linear projection of gas consumption is impossible unless the projection is formulated upon trends of fewer than five years. In general, a trend projection correctly predicts the direction of change in all forecasts, except at "turning points," like the year 1944 in Figure 4.4 and 1956 in Figure 4.5. Such critical points pose the greatest challenge to trend forecasting.

Use of trend projection is also limited by the fact that the projection merely shows the compound effects of many variables and provides little insight into the effects of specific changes in individual variables such as population, energy price, or the availability of substitutes. With today's rapidly changing energy prices and population growth rates, and the possibilities of energy shortages and implementation of energy conservation measures, it is perilous to base long-range policies, in particular those involving major irreversible commitments, on trend projections which mask the detailed interactions of the component factors.

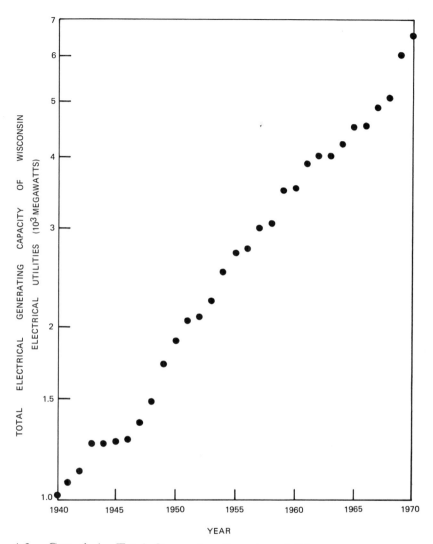

4.3. Growth in Total Generation Capacity of Wisconsin Electrical Utilities. *Source*: "Energy Use in Wisconsin," W. K. Foell and J. E. Rushton.

Econometric Models

When a better understanding of cause and effect is needed, an *econometric model* can be useful. An econometric model explains past economic activity and predicts future economic activity by deriving mathematical equations that express the most probable relationships between sets of economic variables such as disposable

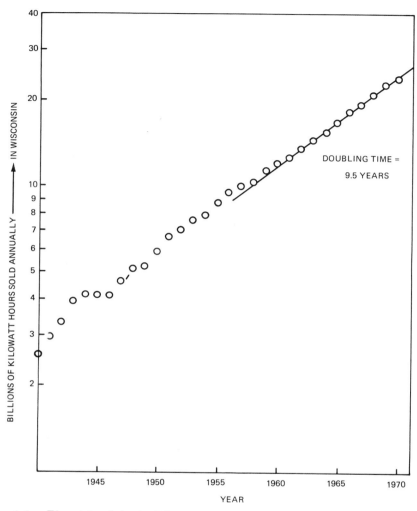

4.4.   Electricity Sales in Wisconsin, 1940-1970. *Source*:   "Energy Use in Wisconsin," W. K. Foell and J. E. Rushton.

income, money stock, and prices of certain goods. The equations are usually those which best describe past behaviors of the variables. If energy demand is included as a pertinent variable, the econometric model can forecast energy demand as a function of other variables.

Econometric models can be very simple, containing only a few variables. But generally, they are fairly complicated. In fact, some econometric models currently used in the United States to study energy demand contain several hundred variables. One econometric model, developed by Mount, Chapman, and Tyrell,[6,7] is being used extensively to forecast electricity demand. The objectives of the MCT model are

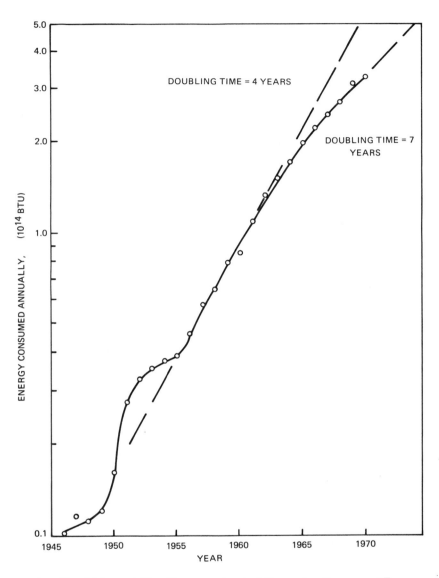

4.5.   Total Natural Gas Consumption in Wisconsin. *Source*:   "Energy Use In Wisconsin," W. K. Foell and J. E. Ruston.

twofold. The first is to determine the relationships between electricity demand and five causal factors—population, income, the price of electricity, substitute fuels, and household appliances. The second goal is to apply these relationships to projections of future demand.

Mount et al. have applied this model to three major electrical consumer

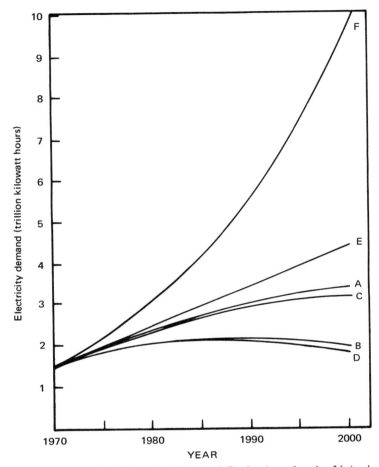

4.6. Alternative Electricty Demand Projections for the United States from the MTC Econometric Model. Projections A, B, C, D & E are based on the assumptions described in Table 4.1. *Source*:   L. D. Chapman, T. J. Tyrell and T. D. Mount, *Science* 178:707 (1972)

classes — residential, commercial, and industrial — for the forty-eight contiguous states in the United States from 1947 to 1970. With their model they made six different electricity demand forecasts, each based on an alternative set of assumptions about the five causal factors (Figure 4.6). The most important assumptions, those specifying electricity price and population, are listed in Table 4.1 along with the resulting electricity demands through the year 2000.

Mount et al. conclude that price of electricity is more important than personal income in determining electricity demand. More significantly, they deduce that if electricity prices continue to increase over the next few years in response to increased fuel costs and other factors, the growth of electricity demand gradually will decline

TABLE 4.1. Electricity Demand Growth and Alternative Assumptions

Case	Population Assumption	Electricity Price Assumption	Electricity Demand (10^{12} kwh)			
			1975	1980	1990	2000
A	BEA[a]	FPC[b]	1.98	2.38	3.01	3.45
B	BEA	Prices double by 2000[c]	1.88	2.07	2.11	2.01
C	ZPG in 2035[d]	FPC	1.98	2.37	2.95	3.29
D	ZPG in 2035[d]	Prices double by 2000	1.88	2.05	2.07	1.91
E	BEA	Constant prices[e]	2.02	2.54	3.56	4.56
F	BEA	Prices decline[f]	2.14	3.05	5.66	9.89

[a] Population estimated to increase 1.4 percent per year by Bureau of Economic Analysis (U.S. Department of Commerce).

[b] The price increase is based upon the FPC estimate given in the 1970 National Power Survey, stating that the real price of electricity will increase by 19 percent between 1970 and 1990.

[c] Price increases annually by 3.33 percent of its 1970 value for 30 years.

[d] Zero population growth is reached in 2035.

[e] 1970 prices are maintained.

[f] This is the deduced price behavior which would be required as input to the model if it were to yield to the FPC demand forecast described by case F. Average prices decline 24 percent from 1970 to 1980 and 12 percent each 10 years thereafter until 2000.

Source: Chapman, Tynell & Mount: *Science* 178: 707 (1972).

from its present rate. No accelerated growth of population or income is expected to offset this price effect. This conclusion contrasts with the National Power Survey's forecast discussed on pp. 37-38. But the judgment of the MCT modelers — that conventional trend projections significantly overestimate the future need for additional generation capacity — is hard to disagree with in light of widely held expectations that electricity prices will increase appreciably in the coming decades.

The MCT model illustrates the major difference between a detailed econometric model and a "mechanical" trend projection — an econometric model can explicitly include the effect of price and other important causal factors. However, econometric models are not completely free of problems. There is considerable debate about the validity of an energy model whose forecasts span more than a decade. The relationships and parameters built into the equations are generally derived from past or current technology and are, consequently, tied to past or current human value systems, technologies, and social institutions. For example, in the MCT model discussed above, the elasticity of electricity demand in relation to price changes was derived from past and current consumer choices. But consumer responses, including their sensitivity to price increases, industrial structures, and other important factors, can change substantially over a ten-year period. Moreover, when new economic or social forces emerge or existing forces change, there may be significant changes in cause-effect relationships. Finally, econometric models are usually cumbersome, costly to develop and operate and require continual updating and modification by highly trained professionals. Nevertheless, if used with good statistical data and theoretical understanding, econometrics can make a major contribution to energy forecasting.

Scenario-Building and Simulation Modeling

When it is necessary to forecast behavior of a system whose internal relationships are subject to change, neither trend projections nor econometric models can be used with confidence. In such cases, the scenario-building technique may be the best approach. Like the plot of a stage play, the modeler's scenario describes a postulated sequence of events which trace out in time the behavior of a system. Scenario-building is the detailed examination of the likelihood and consequences of alternative assumptions about the future. For example, a set of scenarios might describe a world in which (1) energy prices rise rapidly and pollution is difficult to control, (2) energy is inexpensive and pollution easy to control, and (3) various intermediate cases. After a set of alternative assumptions has been selected, their implications are analyzed rigorously. While there is no inherent limitation on the number of scenarios that can be explored quantitatively, lack of manpower and time do impose a practical limit.[8]

Because of these limitations, simulation models which use computers to solve a large number of equations have become an important outgrowth of scenario-building. Once the basic structures of the scenario are built, a modern digital computer can evaluate rapidly the consequences of a large number of different assumptions. This makes it possible to systematically determine the importance of variations in assumptions. For example, the assumption that there will be an increased preference for residential electric heating has no specific implications for future generating capacity unless the number of electrically heated homes is quantified. However, a simulation study covering a range of assumptions about population growth, family size, preferences between rural, urban, single family and apartment living units, rate of demolition of old housing units, house insulation standards, and other facts, could give an overall picture of the potential effects of the increased use of electric heat on future electricity needs.

Simulation models are powerful tools in assessing behavior of very complex systems such as ecosystems, urban systems, and energy systems. For example, Forester[9,10] and Meadows et al.[11] have built models which attempt to describe the structure and dynamic behavior of global natural resource sytems, and the interdependencies of these systems with other sectors of industrialized society. Systems simulation is suited to these studies for several reasons. First, it can cope with the "historical quality" of such systems, that is, their dependence upon past as well as present events. It can handle "time-delay" effects such as the lag between a pollutant's generation and its appearance in another part of the ecosystem. It also can handle "inertia" effects such as the way in which massive capital investments in existing industrial facilities effectively block rapid implementation of technological improvements.

Second, the simulation model can describe the feedback interactions between components of a system. For example, in an energy system, the model can register the effect, through the pricing system, which pollution abatement costs have on energy demand.

Third, simulation can mathematically treat nonlinear components of the system, such as the feedback system described above where the rising price of energy may *not* be directly proportional to the rising cost of pollution abatement. Thus the simulation model, which shows changes in relationships of the components, goes beyond the econometric model which merely calculates changes in the numerical value of components.

The simulation approach also is not without drawbacks and limitations, however. To handle a complex system, simulation modeling requires the use of a modern computer facility with its technical personnel. More important, it requires individuals with a knowledge of both modeling techniques (and model limitations) and the important characteristics of the resource system being modeled. It goes without saying that the results of systems simulation cannot be better than the assumptions built into the model.

A current example of a large-scale simulation study is the Wisconsin State Energy Model, the product of an interdisciplinary research group at the University of Wisconsin. The model analyzes the demand, conversion, transport, utilization, and environmental impact of all forms of energy within five "possible futures" postulated for the state of Wisconsin. Information on the state's energy usage is computer programmed in a mathematical form that simulates the energy system and its relationship to other characteristics of the state. For example, electricity demand forecasts, prerequisites for the installation of additional electrical generation capacity in Wisconsin, are calculated by the modelers under a wide range of assumptions including state population, economic growth, consumer preferences, and energy conservation measures. Unlike trend projection forecasts, which show only the total effect of many variables, the simulation model permits the study of *specific assumptions* about each causal factor.

With the model, "energy scenarios" have been developed for Wisconsin through the year 2000.[12] Figures 4.7 through 4.10 show the electricity demands, by sector, for each scenario developed in the study. The assumptions of the five scenarios are as follows:

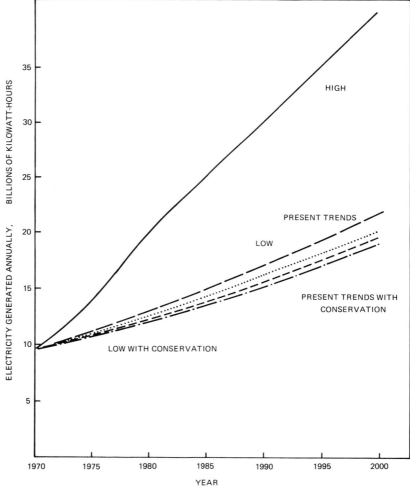

4.7. Electricity Generated for Wisconsin Residential Use. *Source:* "Final Environmental Impact Statement for Columbia Generating Station of the Wisconsin Power and Light Co.," State of Wisconsin Department of Natural Resources, November 1973.

Scenario I, Present Trends. Assumes a continuation of present trends or status quo in:

> appliance purchase or installation;
> old home conversions to electric heating;
> new homes built with electric heating;
> destruction of old housing units;
> industiral production and commercial sales.

Scenario II, High Demand. Assumes a higher-than-present electricity demand based on the following changes:

> all new homes and converted homes have electric heat;
> all current types of appliances are owned by 99 percent of state households by 1990;

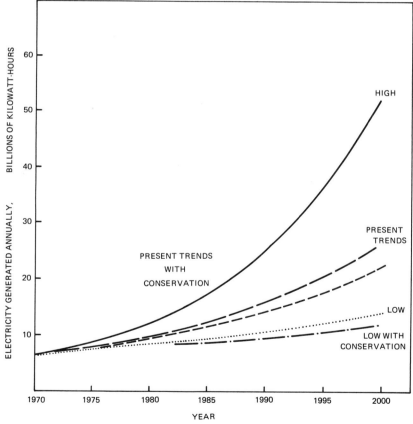

4.8. Electricity Generated for Wisconsin Industrial Use. *Source:* "Final Environmental Impact Statement for Columbia Generating Station of Wisconsin Power and Light Company," State of Wisconsin Department of Natural Resources, November 1973.

growth rates of industrial and commercial activity are set at the highest
historical value of the past 15 years;
energy intensiveness of commercial and industrial sectors is set at highest
historical value of the past 15 years;
energy intensiveness of commercial and industrial sectors is set at highest
value of past 15 years.

Scenario III, Low Demand. Assumes a lower-than-present electricity demand
based on the following changes:

gas maintains current high fraction of use in new and converted homes;

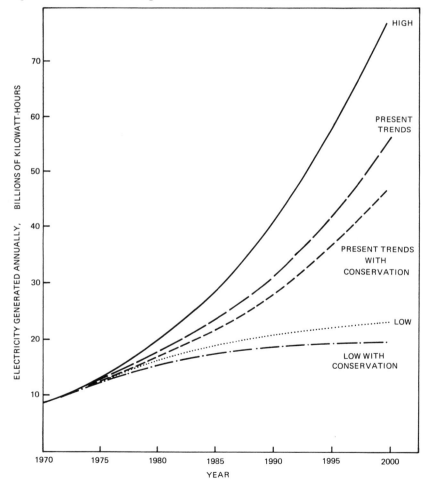

4.9. Electricity Generated for Wisconsin Commercial Use.
Source: "Final Environmental Impact Statement of the Columbia
Generating Station of Wisconsin Power and Light Company," State of
Wisconsin Department of Natural Resources, November 1973.

the number of households owning each electric appliance is limited to
expected 1980 levels;

growth rates of industrial and commercial activity are at moderate
historical levels;

energy intensiveness of industrial and commercial sectors levels off by 1980.

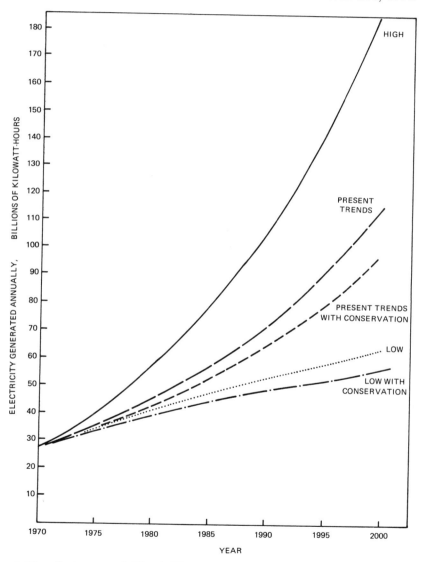

4.10. Estimates of Total Electricity Generated for Wisconsin Use.
Source: "Final Environmental Impact Statement of the Columbia
Generating Station of the Wisconsin Power and Light Company," State of
Wisconsin Department of Natural Resources, November 1973.

Scenarios IV and V, Energy Conservation. Assumes the following conservation measures are implemented in Scenarios I and II:

> all new homes have the "econometric optimum" amount of insulation;[13]
> new air conditioners are more efficient (10 BTU/Watt-hour than the present average conditioner (6 BTU/Watt-hour);
> industrial and commercial conservation measures result in 5 percent energy savings by 1980, 10 percent by 1990 and 15 percent by 2000.[14]

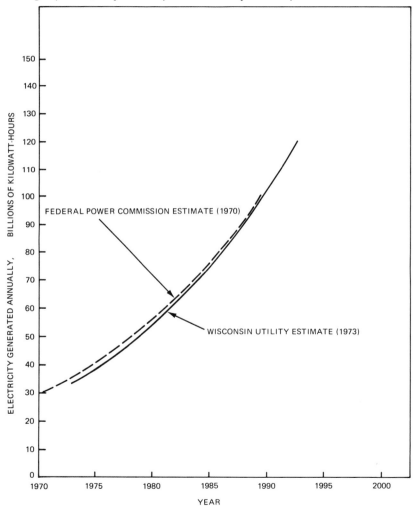

4.11. Comparison of Estimates of Total Electricty Generated for Wisconsin Use. *Source:* "Final Environmental Impact Statement of the Columbia Generating Station of the Wisconsin Power and Light Company," State of Wisconsin Department of Natural Resources, November 1973.

The energy curves representing each scenario in Figures 4.7 through 4.10 show notable divergence, particularly over the long term. By 1985 there is already a 25 percent difference between the postulated high and low demand cases. By the year 2000, the difference has increased by more than a factor of two.

The energy savings of Scenarios IV and V present only a partial picture. There is an accompanying reduction in required generating capacity which offers even greater savings. This reduction is due to the postulated introduction of high efficiency air conditioners and improved efficiency in industrial and commercial processes. Although air conditioners operate only a small fraction of the year, they contribute substantially to the peak demands and therefore to total required capacity. More detailed studies with the state model have indicated that with improved air conditioners, the required capacity for the 1980 summer could be reduced by about 530 MWe. This is an amount slightly more than the output of Point Beach Nuclear Unit I, the largest nuclear plant operating in Wisconsin in 1973. The savings in the year 2000 would amount to a reduction in required summer capacity of approximately 980 MWe, or almost the equivalent of Point Beach Units 1 and 2.

It is interesting to compare the total energy demand curves of the five scenarios with two energy curves (Figure 4.11) derived from current government and utility forecasts. One curve in Figure 4.11 is based on forecasts presented in the Federal Power Commission's 1970 National Power Survey.[15] The other derives from data supplied by Wisconsin utilities at energy hearings of the Wisconsin Public Services Commission, July 1973. The two forecasts are not independent since the FPC forecast is based primarily upon information supplied by the utilities. According to the PSC hearings, trend projection was the basic tool used in making these forecasts. It is significant that the FPC and Wisconsin utility forecasts lie in the vicinity of the high demand scenario for most of the time period covered.

A state energy model such as the one described above cannot give absolute predictions for the state's electricity future, but it can provide insight into possible futures. It can also indicate the response of the total energy system to changes in factors which influence electricity demand.[16]

Some Concluding Comments on Models

Though forecasting is perhaps the most widely recognized application of resource models, there are two other important uses of models in resource management: (1) assessment of the overall behavior of a resource system; and (2) improvement of the management of the resource.

In an assessment of overall behavior, the model provides a mechanism for putting together many different pieces in one large picture. For example, a model which relates environmental protection costs to energy price and demand can help evaluate the impact of proposed environmental standards. The "what would happen if . . . ?" procedure is useful in the assessment process.

Optimization of management is a common goal of models, particularly in industry. For example, a group of petroleum refineries might attempt to increase their production with minimum cost and within the constraints of product demand and resource supply.[17] On a much broader scale, models can be applied to the problem of how to maximize a nation's economic activity and yet stay within the limits posed by resource availability and environmental standards.[18, 19]

Regardless of the kind of model used, the ultimate goal of modeling efforts is to establish a better basis for policy decisions leading to a long-term improvement in the human condition.[20] However, as many modelers have been quick to perceive, improvement in methodology alone does not improve policy-making. Even the best resource analysis often fails to dissuade decision-makers from their pre-conceptions.[21] Many scientists, ecologists, and others who study and model natural resource systems are beginning to recognize that describing the behavior of a system is only half the goal; they must also communicate their findings to the political arena. Only through feedback through the public testing of policies and options and through the revision of models in the light of real events, can the model ultimately demonstrate its value.

References

1. R. J. Thierauf and R. A. Grosse, *Decision Making Through Operations Research* (New York: Wiley and Sons, 1970), p. 14.
2. These feedback mechanisms are the basis for the biocybernetic technology discussed below in Chapter 10.
3. C. J. Walters, "Systems Ecology: The Systems Approach and Mathematical Models in Ecology," in E. P. Odum, *Fundamentals of Ecology*, 3rd ed. (Philadelphia: W. B. Saunders, 1971), p. 278.
4. Walters, "Systems Ecology," *Fundamentals of Ecology*, p. 277.
5. W. K. Foell and James Rushton, "Energy Use in Wisconsin: A Survey of Energy Flow in the State of Wisconsin," Working Paper No. 4, Institute for Environmental Studies (Madison: University of Wisconsin, 1972), p.34.
6. T. D. Mount, L. D. Chapman, and T. J. Tyrell, *Electricity Demand in the United States: An Econometric Analysis*, Oak Ridge National Laboratory Rept. NSF-EP-49 (Oak Ridge, Tenn.: 1973).
7. L. D. Chapman, T. J. Tyrell, and T. D. Mount, "Electricity Demand Growth and the Energy Crisis," *Science* 178: 703-708 (November 1972).
8. R. L. Gordon, "Scenarios for Energy — Environment Policy-Making," Proceedings of Summer Workshop on Energy, Environment, and Long-term Decisions, Organization for Economic Cooperation and Development, Paris, August 1973.
9. J. W. Forrester, *Urban Dynamics* (Cambridge, Mass.: MIT Press, 1969), pp. 12-37.
10. J. W. Forrester, *World Dynamics* (Cambridge, Mass.: Wright-Allen Press, 1971), pp.13-30.
11. Donella H. Meadows, Dennis L. Meadows, Jørgen Randers, and William W. Behrens III, *The Limits to Growth* (New York: Universe, 1972), pp. 26-29.

12. W. K. Foell, "Simulation Modeling of Energy Systems: A Decision-Making Tool," Summer Workshop on Energy, Paris, August 1973.

13. See Table 7.2 and accompanying text in Chapter 7 for more discussion of energy conservation through improved insulation.

14. The latter savings potential, probably a conservative estimate, is based on information developed by the U.S. Office of Emergency Preparedness in *The Potential for Energy Conservation*, Report OEP4102-0009 (Washington, D.C.: 1972).

15. *1970 National Power Survey*, Report by the Federal Power Commission, 4 vol. (Washington, D.C.: U.S. Government Printing Office, 1971), pp. III-2-4 - III-2-7.

16. Though the effects of rising electricity prices have not been treated explicitly in these studies, the MCT model discussed earlier in this chapter indicates the need for further consideration of pricing effects.

17. R.J. Deam and J. Leather, "World Energy Modeling," paper presented to Conference on Energy: Demand, Conservation, and Institutional Problems, at MIT, Cambridge, Mass., February 1973.

18. R. T. Thoss, and H. P. Dollekes, "Energy and Environmental Planning," Summer Workshop on Energy, Paris, August 1973.

19. Y. Shimazu, "Energy Consumption and Limits to Growth in Japan," Summer Workshop on Energy, Paris, August 1973.

20. Further discussion of these and other modeling methods and uses can be found in the following: Milton Searl, ed., *Energy Modeling: Working Papers for a Seminar on Energy Modeling*, Working Paper of Resources for the Future, EN-1 (Washington, D.C.: March 1973); N. Siemens, C. H. Marting, and F. Greenwood, *Operations Research* (New York: Free Press, 1973); S. E. Elmaghraby, "The Role of Modeling in Industrial Engineering Design," *Journal of Industrial Engineering* 19:292-305 (June 1968).

21. See discussion in Chapter 2 on bad decisions for good reasons, pp. 20-21.

5.   Faustian and Other Bargains

When shortages develop unexpectedly in supplies of crucial resources or energy, the chance increases for resource policy decisions to be made in a shortsighted way, with possibly long-lasting, regrettable effects. Such decisions are excusable, if at all, only in conditions of unforeseeable shortages. It is inexcusable when a resource is seen in advance to be dwindling and there is lead time sufficient for the invention of thoughtful policies. Unfortunately, there is a tendency, even when adequate time exists, for a strong minority, or even individuals, to push their "obvious solutions" onto decision-makers, at the same time discounting or disregarding criticisms or alternatives. This problem is analyzed in the present chapter.

Risks and Payments

Every human use of a resource requires a payment or sacrifice. This is true even on the most basic level. The farm lad who covets an apple high in a tree may "pay" for that apple in a variety of ways. First, he will make a very real payment on the spot in the form of the energy he expends in climbing the tree. Second, he will take risks. One might be that of falling out of the tree. Another might be that from his vantage point on the ground he cannot be sure that the apple does not contain a worm. If the boy actually acquired the apple and ate it with satisfaction, we can assume that the expenditure of energy and the risk-taking were worth it. But we can only know this by hindsight; that is, we can conclude the boy profited from the transaction if he had enough energy to reach the apple, if he did not come crashing out of the tree, and if the apple was in fact delicious and worm-free.

Unfortunately, not all trade-offs in resource use can be seen with such clarity. Insofar as resource use is part of functioning, dynamic economic or technological systems, elements of resource use become difficult to define. Thus, in the totality of human resource use, the boy becomes all of global society, reflecting its every individual and collective and conflicting interest. The apple also loses definition; it

60

can become as nebulous as a "high standard of living," as abstract as "security," or as complex as "gross national product." The payment or sacrifice made for the use of resources also becomes obscure. Thus, the price, or actual cash payment made for a service or commodity, does not include all social or environmental costs, costs which economists call *externalities*. Portions of the payment for the use of a resource may be delayed to later generations, as in the case of a polluted river, or obscured, as in the unproved effects on health of long-term exposure to low levels of sulfur dioxide in urban atmospheres. Externalities, by definition, are costs not paid by the immediate resource user or consumer, but ultimately paid for in an indirect form by both the consumer *and others*.

The use of a resource by any given technology may have unforeseen consequences. Once again, whether the resource use was worth it can be judged only by hindsight. This goes far to explain the upwelling of popular environmental concern of the late 1960s and early 1970s. Large segments of the public came to understand that much pollution and environmental degradation could be attributed to the unwanted and often unanticipated by-products of resource use and processing. Thus, ecology and other sciences revealed that phosphate laundry detergents were "fertilizing" freshwater bodies to the point of accelerated eutrophication; that the smog of urban atmospheres was the result of exhausts from thousands of automobiles; that nitrites produced by widespread application of agricultural fertilizers were threatening the quality of ground water.[1]

Ironically, even when later knowledge or experience shows that the "payment" for some resource use is far greater than the advertised "price," and even when the true payment, including social and environmental costs, becomes widely publicized, large populations still willingly pay it. That is partly because they have grown dependent upon the technologies. They make investments of money or changes in living patterns based upon a technology such as the laundry machine that works at optimum performance only with detergents. Other examples come to mind. The payment Americans make for their automobile-based transportation system is far greater than the price of the car, the labor that produced it, and the gasoline that powers it. It also includes the loss of environmental quality and healthfulness through highway construction and air and noise pollution. More dramatically, it annually extracts a random sacrifice of 50,000 American lives. Yet Americans pay it. Some must pay it because no alternatives exist, especially for commuting from suburbia to the city center. The payment for smoking cigarettes is also far greater than the "price" of a package, including taxes paid to the state. It is an unknown loss of life and health through lung cancer and other diseases. Still, many people take the risk, and many of these make the delayed, final payment.[2] Finally, there are the residents of "smeltertown" — Tacoma, Washington — who, even after being warned of the dangers of exposure to arsenic from the copper smelters, choose to remain there with their children because of their jobs.[3]

According to René Dubos and Barbara Ward:

> The costs cannot be avoided. The citizen pays either as consumer or as taxpayer or as victim. The political and economic problems raised by this inexorable and unavoidable price spring from the fact that different citizens are involved in the

problem in quite different degrees. The taxpayer may be out of reach of the major pollutions and have no direct incentive to clean them up. Yet poorer citizens can hardly welcome an increase in consumer prices for daily necessities even though they might be glad of cleaner air. The calculus of who shall pay for what improvement is *the* political issue at the core of any policy designed to deal with hidden subsidies and external diseconomies that underlie many of the present methods of satisfying economic needs.[4]

Thus, the "payment" extracted by resource use can take a variety of forms: the cash "price," consumption of energy, loss of environmental quality, loss of property, health, or life. It can even be the sacrifice of an abstract value or ideal held to be of unquantifiable value. In its simplest form this might be the radio of one's neighbor drowning out the morning call of a cardinal in one's cedar tree. This is a collision of values, and whether the neighbors can negotiate the relative value of the morning gossip show versus the cardinal's song may depend upon how both value "neighborliness." In another case, it is difficult to put a monetary value on the beauty of a landscape threatened by the advance of urban development. Therefore, the decision on whether the landscape will be destroyed may not rest on a discussion of costs and benefits, but on whether the constituency which admires the landscape knows how to use political power more effectively than the constituency in favor of the highway, or the airport, or the subdivision.

The Unseen Costs of Nuclear Power

If the technology for using or extracting a resource is new, its application widespread, and the existing social and scientific institutions inadequate for a comprehensive review of potential side effects, both quantifiable and intangible, then the need for foresight can be very great. The example here is the widespread use of nuclear reactors for the generation of electricity in the United States. In 1967, the United States had a few small nuclear generators, totaling 1,000 megawatts of capacity. In April 1973, the United States had thirty operating nuclear generators, totaling 15,500 megawatts. That year, the U.S. Atomic Energy Commission forecast that by the year 2000 the nation would have 1,200,000 megawatts of nuclear generating capacity of which more than 400,000 megawatts would come from liquid metal fast breeder reactors.[5]

The case for nuclear power is a strong one. As of 1973, there were perceived shortages of alternative sources of energy. A shortage of domestic petroleum supplies increased the need to search offshore for oil and build the Alaskan pipeline, steps involving high environmental risk. The Arabian action to shut off the oil exports to the West revealed the practical extent of U.S. reliance upon foreign reserves. Furthermore, although there was abundant coal in the United States, its use was restricted by the environmental problems of strip mining and the air pollution produced by burning. Against this background, nuclear power seemed to offer an all but inexhaustible supply of clean power for the future.

While the nuclear power stations were planned, purchased, or under construction, and a few were generating power, debate continued about their environmental impact. The main concerns were the amounts of heated water they would return to natural waterways and their radiological safety. John W. Gofman and Arthur R. Tamplin, research associates at the Lawrence Radiation Laboratory, Livermore, California, attracted widespread publicity with their contentions that even minute levels of radioactivity were dangerous.[6] Henry Kendall, of Massachusetts Institute of Technology, and others joined in the questioning of whether the safety systems of generators already constructed could prevent massive releases of radioactivity.

Such arguments, however, were natural science problems, theoretically subject to quantification. They came from natural scientists, biochemists, nuclear physicists, and others, who were dealing with potential "payments" of a tangible nature: if a given level of radioactivity was inadvertently released, then x persons would die and y dollars of property damage would occur. This was an added cost quite like the payment in lives extracted by the national reliance upon the automobile transportation system. If the numbers had not been filled in yet, it was because there was disagreement over the effects of low level radiation.

But there were intangible costs as well, and, while these may have been considered by promoters and developers of nuclear technology for many years, they remained to be clearly identified in laymen's terms and more widely broadcast. It was Alvin Weinberg, director of the Oak Ridge National Laboratory, who finally delivered the message to the public in a speech, later published as an article in *Science* magazine, called "Social Institutions and Nuclear Energy."[7]

The Faustian Bargain

In his article, Weinberg identified an unusual social issue which revealed to some that an increased reliance upon nuclear power might constitute a direct threat to a cherished western value; that is, to traditional concepts of individual freedom. He called it a "Faustian bargain," in which "society" was to pay dearly for an inexhaustible source of power, much like the bargain struck by the legendary Faust, who sold his soul to the Devil in return for temporal influence.

According to Weinberg, the United States, committed today to more than 100 million kilowatts of nuclear power, may be generating electricity at a rate of 1 billion kilowatts by the year 2000. If such projections materialize, the United States will have to isolate about 27,000 megacuries of radioactive wastes which will be generating about 100,000 kilowatts of heat by 2000.

"Of these, the 239 P [Plutonium 239] with a half-life of 24,400 years will be dangerous for perhaps 200,000 years," Weinberg said. (A half-life is the time required for half of the atoms of a radioactive substance to disintegrate.)

Weinberg reviewed the proposed methods for dealing with such wastes, including those of W. Bennett Lewis, of Atomic Energy of Canada, Inc., who has argued that once man commits himself to nuclear power, he commits himself to "essentially perpetual surveillance." Lewis, said Weinberg, favored storing wastes at radioactive operations centers, to be reworked and recycled as emerging technology permits. Weinberg favored putting the wastes "forever out of contact with the biosphere." In this regard, he described the Atomic Energy Commission's activities to develop a large scale disposal in abandoned salt mines in Kansas.

> The great advantage of the salt method . . . is that our commitment to surveillance in the case of salt is minimal. All we have to do is prevent man from intruding, rather than keeping a priesthood that forever reworks the wastes or guards the vaults. And if the civilization should falter, which would mean, among other things, that we abandon nuclear power altogether, we can be almost (but not totally) assured that no harm would befall our recidivist descendants of the distant future.

Thus did Weinberg arrive at his conclusion:

> We nuclear people have made a Faustian bargain with society. On the one hand we offer — in the catalytic nuclear burner [the breeder reactor] — an inexhaustible source of energy . . . But the price that we demand of society for this magical energy source is both a vigilance and a longevity of our social institutions that we are quite unaccustomed to. . . .
> We make two demands. The first . . . is that we exercise in nuclear technology the very best techniques and that we use people of high expertise and purpose. . . . The second demand is less clear, and I hope it may prove to be unnecessary. This is the demand for longevity in human institutions. We have relatively little problem dealing with wastes if we can assume always that there will be intelligent people around to cope with eventualities we have not thought of. If the nuclear parks that I mention are permanent features of our civilization, then we presumably have the social apparatus, and possibly the sites, for dealing with our wastes indefinitely. But even our salt mines may require some small measure of surveillance if only to prevent men in the future from drilling holes in the burial grounds.

Finally, Weinberg asked:

> Is mankind prepared to exert the eternal vigilance needed to ensure proper and safe operation of its nuclear energy system? This admittedly is a significant commitment that we ask of society. What we offer in return, an all but infinite source of relatively cheap and clean energy, seems to me to be well worth the price.[8]

Those familiar with the German legend know that Faust sells his soul to the Devil in return for temporal power and influence. Is this the price "society" must pay for inexhaustible energy? Although he did not say so in his article, Weinberg believes it is not. In a speech at the University of Wisconsin early in 1973,[9] he stated his preference for Goethe's version of the legend in which Goethe had Faust redeemed at last, thereby cheating the Devil.

These are concepts of time seldom before put forward by scientists: Weinberg uses phrases such as "permanent features," "eternal vigilance," "forever out of contact." He is discussing the need for permanence, not only of manmade physical systems, but of social institutions. If Weinberg is asking for social institutions to watch over the dangerous lifespan of only that Plutonium 239 which will have accumulated by the year 2000, such institutions must survive whatever social and natural upheavals occur in the next 200,000 years. Yet man is a species with a written history of, at the outside limit, 7,000 years. In that time, hundreds of governments and other social institutions have appeared and vanished. The longest standing physical features of any size constructed by man are the Egyptian pyramids, which have endured for 4,500 years. One of the most enduring social institutions is the Roman Catholic Church, of nearly 2,000 years' standing.

How do the imperatives of the Faustian bargain relate to the social institutions of the United States?

It is not necessary here to trace the body of law built on the foundations of the Constitution of the United States and the other main source document of the Republic, the Declaration of Independence. These documents embody concepts of individual and social freedom that much of the nation believes to be valid. They set limits beyond which government theoretically may not intrude on individual privacy, mobility, and matters of conscience. Are the issues put forward by Weinberg an extension of or a contradiction to the ideas of those documents?

In some fundamental ways, they seem directly opposed. Weinberg speaks of the need for people of high expertise and purpose to be ever present in nuclear technology. He notes that some men in nuclear science speak of "priesthoods," which can be taken to mean an elite corps of high competence and high motivation to provide "eternal" watchfulness over nuclear systems. One can visualize here a world in which all factions continue to compete, often angrily and violently, for the usual reasons, racial, economic, religious, and political — a perpetuation of history so far, but with one major new restraint: the conflict must not touch at any cost, even that of the "due process" concept, the priesthood or other institutions charged with securing radioactive wastes.

Furthermore, it should be remembered that "priesthoods" — that is, elitist, disciplined classes of people who accept as their responsibility the long-range welfare of their constituencies — are corruptible. Cases are not uncommon: quack physicians, scientists who permit their data to be prostituted by narrow interests, clerics who break vows, journalists who avoid controversies, military leaders who inappropriately intrude upon purely political issues, lawyers who commit crimes. No true priesthood has ever existed if invulnerability and incorruptibility are essential characteristics.

Short of achieving human perfection, nuclear priests, over infinite time, will be successful only relatively. *If* the demands of the bargain are absolute and with no provision for failure, then those imperfect priests who fail, fail absolutely. In spite of this possibility and the uncertainties of nuclear safety, Weinberg looks to social forums to provide the extra vigilance needed for safe operation of a nuclear energy system.

Weinberg's bargain is based on the perfection on schedule of the breeder reactor. However, insofar as there were already thirty operating nuclear power plants in the United States in 1973, the imperatives of that bargain were already upon society to some degree. Yet there was little evidence that the social commitments — the longevity of social institutions and whatever degree of priesthood was needed —

were understood except by Weinberg and a few others. Certainly not by the general public. The one institution wherein might reside a budding priesthood and source of guidance — the Atomic Energy Commission — was under attack by environmental advocates and others for allegedly failing to meet the first standard of any priesthood, that of regulatory disinterest. Critics often pointed to its dual and seemingly conflicting roles of regulating and promoting nuclear power. Thus, it remained for Weinberg, a nuclear scientist, to identify even abstractly for the public the more crucial issue.

Technology's Other Bargains

It is significant that when Weinberg speaks of "we nuclear people" and "society," it is as though they were separate parties negotiating a contract. Other technologists tend to propose, plan, or put into action new technologies with little assessment or even recognition of possible detriment to the "other party"; social or environmental side effects are ignored. Barry Commoner accuses such men of narrow vision. Had the developers of synthetic detergents gone beyond questions of the products' effectiveness as washing agents, he argues, the developers might have found that large amounts of phosphate detergents in waterways would be harmful. Tunnel vision also can be blamed for the unintended consequences of pesticides, the automobile, plastics in landfill sites, the Aswan Dam, nuclear bombs, and so on, Commoner says.[10]

Even when "society" is considered, it is often perceived as the only element of the two, society or technology, that must be altered to keep the two parties compatible. This is the theme of *Century of Mismatch*,[11] by Simon Ramo, former vice chairman of the board of TRW, Inc., and research associate at the California Institute of Technology. Ramo contends there is an imbalance, a mismatch between technological advance on the one hand and social "maturing" on the other.

"The appropriate action is to work at speeding up social advance and improving the selection of priorities for technological investment," says Ramo.

Like Weinberg, Ramo presents the demands technology makes upon society as imperatives:

> The machines require, for their optimum performance, certain patterns of society. We too have preferred arrangements. But we want what the machines can furnish, and so we must compromise. We must alter the rules of society so that we and they can be compatible.[12]

There is yet another, more dramatic, claim by a technologist that society must change to meet the imperatives of technology. In this case, B. F. Skinner, Edgar Pierce Professor of Psychology at Harvard University, in *Beyond Freedom and Dignity*,[13] argues that people ought to abandon concepts of personal freedom, personal dignity, and individual responsibility to meet the imperatives of present and emerging technology. He begins:

> In trying to solve the terrifying problems that face us in the world today, we naturally turn to the things we do best. We play from strength, and our strength is science and technology. To contain a population explosion, we look for better methods of birth control. Threatened by a nuclear holocaust, we build bigger deterrent forces and anti-ballistic-missile systems. We try to stave off world famine with new foods and better ways of growing them. Improved sanitation and medicine will, we hope, control disease, better housing and transportation will solve the problems of the ghettos, and new ways of reducing or disposing of waste will stop the pollution of the environment.[14]

However, says Skinner, "things grow steadily worse and it is disheartening to find that technology itself is increasingly at fault."

Thus, Skinner begins his argument on a foundation quite like that which underlies the recurring themes of environmental protection. Like Commoner, he has attacked technology. He continues:

> It is not enough to "use technology with a deeper understanding of human issues," or to "dedicate technology to man's spiritual needs," or to "encourage technologists to look at human problems." . . . What we need is a technology of behavior. We could solve our problems quickly enough if we could adjust the growth of the world's population as precisely as we adjust the course of a spaceship, or improve agriculture and industry with some of the confidence with which we accelerate high-energy particles, or move toward a peaceful world with something like the steady progress with which physics has approached absolute zero (even though both remain presumably out of reach). But a behavioral technology comparable in power and precision to physical and biological technology is lacking, and those who do not find the very possibility ridiculous are more likely to be frightened by it than reassured. That is how far we are from "understanding human issues" in the sense in which physics and biology understand their fields, and how far we are from preventing the catastrophe toward which the world seems to be inexorably moving.[15]

"And as to technology," he says, "we have made immense strides in controlling the physical and biological worlds, but our practices in government, education, and much of economics, though adapted to very different conditions, have not greatly improved."

Before Skinner undertakes his challenge of the concepts of freedom and dignity and describes his "technology of behavior," based on years of experiments with operant conditioning using positive reinforcement,[16] he leaves us with the thought that the technology of behavior may possibly be the "only way to solve our problems."[17]

Now we have two Faustian bargains, Weinberg's and Skinner's. Both offer a technology which promises mankind comfort, security, well-being, and happiness. But society must pay for their use. For Weinberg's inexhaustible source of energy, society will contribute eternal watchfulness and stable social institutions. For Skinner's solution of all problems of war, pollution, population, and disease, society will surrender its concepts of freedom and personal dignity.

In his novel, *Walden Two*,[18] Skinner shows how his social stucture would work.

In fact, *Walden Two* could be a description of the society dictated by the Weinberg technology. Among other things, it provides for a "permanent social structure."[19] Within the structure, it would seem a simple problem to provide competent men of high motive (priesthoods) to cope with environmental contamination (such as radioactive wastes) and any other contingency that arises in adjusting society to technology, or the reverse. In *Walden Two*, "planners" are in fact at work on such problems.

Are We Ready to Bargain?

Is present-day man ready for either Skinnerian or Weinbergian technology? Each Fourth of July, Americans are flooded with reminders that "freedom" and "dignity" are basic tenets of their society. The civil rights movement of the 1960s demanded equal standing before the law, equal opportunity, full freedom of expression, all those freedoms that much of the United States population believed it already enjoyed. Issues articulated in the Watergate affair were whether concepts of separation of powers and access to public information — both measures conceived to be safeguards against tyrannies — had been undermined.

It is not important here to raise the question of whether man is, in fact, free. What is important is the fact that uncounted millions of people *believe* themselves either to be free or to be in pursuit of freedom.

What Skinner has proposed is a society which works for its survival through a technology of behavior, that is, an application of the principles of science to accomplish the goal of survival. As a technology it is ethically neutral; that is, its use can be for social or selfish purposes. However, as we have seen, many current problems, particularly environmental degradation, are unanticipated, unwanted side effects of a neutral technology.

If society agreed to a Skinnerian world or if such a world were coercively imposed by some emerging new imperative, such as the need to sequester radioactive wastes forever, and it was found to have some unforeseen drawback, could there be a retreat from it? We have seen how difficult it has been for people to sever their dependence upon high phosphate detergents, a relatively small technology, after the true payment became known. If the concepts of "freedom" and "dignity" were found to have survival value after all, could society retreat from the "technology of behavior?"

It is directly to the point here to note that there is evidence from scientific observation that individuals ought to be free to perform in unpredictable, disorderly ways. There is survival value in such disorder, in spontaneous behavior. Van R. Potter, Leonardo Scholar and professor of oncology at the University of Wisconsin, has written:

> I wish to emphasize the notion that disorder is built in, that it is maintained by Darwinian natural selection, that it is an essential part of the biological system, and that our aim should not be to eliminate it, but rather to recognize it for what it is

and to harness it creatively in a continuous tension and balance with order. Trouble and misery are in part the price we pay for the disorder that is necessary for evolution to occur. It can be argued that in biological evolution nature has achieved a kind of "ordered disorder" to achieve survival in the natural milieu. What I proclaim is that in cultural evolution we should do likewise.[20]

George Wald, professor of biology at Harvard University, states:

> Each of us possesses a unique composition that changes from moment to moment. Each of us carries also a unique genetic complement that, what with recessives that are not expressed and dominant genes that for some unknown reason withhold their effects, remains to a large degree hidden. All of us bear hereditary potentials that we know nothing about and will never find anything about. Furthermore, we store history, a continuous flow of experience. When the time comes to make a decision, to exercise what we call free will, to choose — when that time comes, the self that exercises free will is, I think, that unique private self, that unique product of the unique composition, genetics and history, all to a degree unknown. At that moment no one can predict the outcome, neither an outsider nor the person making the decision, because no one has the requisite information. So I should say that the essence of free will is not a failure of determinism but a failure of predictability.[21]

Thus, "freedom" in biology can be equated with diversity, disorder, individuality, unpredictability. It is a long recognized ecological principle that diversity in any biotic community contributes to stability.[22] If scientific disagreement does exist, then, on the question of the value of freedom, Faustian bargains such as those elucidated by both Weinberg and Skinner constitute option-closing on a grand scale.

Returning to the apple and the boy, under the conditions presented by Weinberg and Skinner the boy is seen as starving and the apple is the only one on the tree. Whether it has fatally toxic worms working inside it is quite beside the point. The boy must take the risks.

Do Skinner and Weinberg require our urgent attention? It is doubtful in Skinner's case. While history offers examples of official attempts at psychological control for political reasons, Skinner does not threaten coercion. He has written books of compelling intellectual interest, but his books contain no recommendation to decision-makers for applying operant conditioning to large populations.

Weinberg's case is different. First, he is qualified to speak about the physical problems of nuclear waste disposal. Second, the imperatives of the Faustian bargain are present and the urgency of meeting them grows with the installation of each new nuclear power plant.

Weinberg says that the decisions presented by the bargain — in which mankind provides permanent social institutions and perpetual watchfulness — are "society's" to make. They transcend science, he says. This implies that there might be alternatives, other apples, perhaps on lower, more easily reached branches. Are there? One might be the cleaning of "dirty" fossil fuels, thereby extending their use and lessening reliance on nuclear power. There seems to be a second alternative immediately available: perfect the long neglected "technology" of recycling and energy conservation, if for no other reason than to move into Faustian bargains more slowly, more cautiously, and after the nature of the sacrifice becomes more clearly understood.

References

1. Barry Commoner, *The Closing Circle* (New York: Knopf, 1971), pp. 66-111.
2. Barbara Ward and René Dubos, *Only One Earth* (New York: Norton, 1972), p. 221.
3. Communication to Leonardo Seminar, May 18, 1973, by Clancy Gordon, professor of biology, University of Montana.
4. Ward and Dubos, *Only One Earth*, p. 49-50.
5. Press Release No. 983, Atomic Energy Commission, Chicago Operations Office, Argonne, Illinois, March 7, 1973.
6. John W. Gofman and Arthur R. Tamplin, *Poisoned Power* (Emmaus, Pa.: Rodale Press, 1971).
7. Alvin W. Weinberg, "Social Institutions and Nuclear Energy," *Science* 177:27-34 (July 7, 1972).
8. Ibid., pp. 33, 34.
9. Alvin Weinberg, "Faustian Bargains in Energy," University of Wisconsin Symposium, February 12, 1973.
10. Commoner, *Closing Circle*, p. 183.
11. Simon Ramo, *Century of Mismatch* (New York: David McKay, 1970).
12. Ibid., p. 12.
13. B.F. Skinner, *Beyond Freedom and Dignity* (New York: Knopf, 1971).
14. Ibid., p. 3.
15. Ibid., pp. 4-5.
16. *Operant Conditioning* is Skinner's term for getting the behavior one wants from another through *positive reinforcements*. When, for example, a pigeon pecks a lever (the desired behavior), it receives a grain of food (the positive reinforcement).
17. Skinner, *Beyond Freedom and Dignity*, pp. 1-23.
18. B. F. Skinner, *Walden Two* (New York: Macmillan, 1972), p. 196.
19. Ibid., p. 196.
20. Van R. Potter, "Disorder as a Built-In Component of Biological Systems: The Survival Imperative," *Zygon*, vol. 6, no. 2, 138-39 (June 1971).
21. George Wald, "Determinancy, Individuality, and the Problem of Free Will," in John R. Platt, ed., *New Views of the Nature of Man* (Chicago: University of Chicago Press, 1965), pp. 36-37.
22. Orie Loucks, "Evolution of Diversity, Efficiency, and Community Stability," *American Zoologist* 10:17-19 (1970); see also The Institute of Ecology, *Man in the Living Environment* (Madison: University of Wisconsin Press, 1971), pp. 112-17.

6.   Resource Use In Conflict

Natural resource policy decisions made within the constraints of existing social organization inevitably contain seeds of conflict. For example, a decision to exploit one highly demanded resource at the expense of another could easily ignite local if not national conflicts between resource users. Indeed, the potential for a resource conflict of serious proportions already exists. The protagonists are the world's suppliers of energy and the world's producers of food.

The Dilemma

In 1973 there was widespread speculation among expert observers[1] that millions of persons in southern Asia and parts of Africa faced famine as a result of drought. This picture was complicated by the fact that the Soviet Union had entered the world grain market and bought American-produced grains that otherwise might have been sold as surpluses to needy countries. Meanwhile, in the United States, the most overfed country in the world in terms of average per capita caloric intake,[2] widespread publicity was given to the prospect of meat and produce shortages. These shortages were manifested primarily as higher food prices, but in some areas as actual insufficiencies. In short, fundamental changes were occurring rapidly in what had been for years a relatively stable agricultural picture. The post-World War II food surpluses were gone. Farmers were commanding higher prices for their products. The United States had developed a policy to use its agricultural capacity to produce foodstuffs for export and thereby to improve its balance of payments.

Simultaneously, there was widespread acknowledgment that the United States faced an energy shortage of unknown duration, brought on by rapidly increasing demand; dwindling cheap, easy-to-get reserves of oil and natural gas; environmental controls; delayed completion of nuclear power plants; and the policies of oil companies and government.

Concern about sulfur dioxide pollution caused electric utilities to turn to low sulfur fuels — natural gas, oil, and some western coals. During 1971, the rate of increase in fuel consumption by utilities was more than ten times higher for oil than for coal, a shift believed to be caused mainly by environmental considerations.[3]

Electrical generation and the huge demand for gasoline and other petroleum products had caused oil imports to steadily rise from 113 million barrels in 1945 to 1.4 billion barrels in 1971.[4]

Meanwhile, pressure had increased for heavier use of coal, a fuel which the United States had in abundance, especially for more use of low sulfur coals.[5] However, in spite of cleaning processes to remove sulfur, the average coal burned in the United States in 1972 still contained approximately 2 percent sulfur.[6]

In this setting, increased demands for both energy and food to meet the needs of a rapidly expanding world pose several potential resource conflicts: (1) a growing reliance on ocean transport of oil will lead to more oil spills which threaten fisheries; (2) strip mining the vast untapped reserves of low sulfur coal under the western Dakotas, eastern Montana, and northeastern Wyoming may destroy wheat lands; and (3) strip mining the traditional reserves of high sulfur coal, still worked intensively in Illinois, Indiana, and Iowa, will disrupt fertile corn, wheat, and soybean lands.

The use of one resource, urgently needed to supply real needs, therefore, can pre-empt the use of another resource, also urgently needed for other but no less real needs. How are decisions to be made? If coal lies under fertile wheat lands and is economically available only through strip mining, how are the relative values of coal and wheat to be weighed? Or, how is the supply of oil to be balanced against the potential destruction of breeding habitats of oysters, shrimp, striped bass, herring, and other fisheries by petroleum pollutants?

Oil Tankers and Marine Fisheries

The conflict between increased oceanic transport of oil and the continued healthy survival of marine fisheries grows relentlessly. Oil pollution in the ocean is already widespread.[7] *Spillage reached 24 million tons a year in 1973.*[8] By 1980, 48 percent of the oil used in the United States may be imported, compared with 29 percent imported in 1972.[9]

It has been argued that supertankers and deepwater terminals for unloading the huge ships will reduce the danger of accidental oil spills. One supertanker of 250,000 dead weight tons can handle a fuel cargo that normally would require 5 traditional tankers of 47,000 DWT.[10] A reliance on supertankers thus would reduce tanker traffic and lower the probability of accidents. However, supertankers will be harder to maneuver, will have more momentum, and will cause larger spills when they do occur.[11] Whether the oil is shipped in large or small tankers, the increased volume being transported will likely increase the oil spilled by some amount.[12] The current environmental debate concerns ways to keep this spillage to a minimum.

Spilled oil is much more likely to harm marine life in inshore areas, such as estuaries, than in the open ocean.[13] More than two-thirds of the food-fish depend on estuaries for shelter, spawning, juvenile rearing, or habitat.[14] The activities involved in construction of deepwater ports and onshore refining plants also may harm inshore marine habitats.

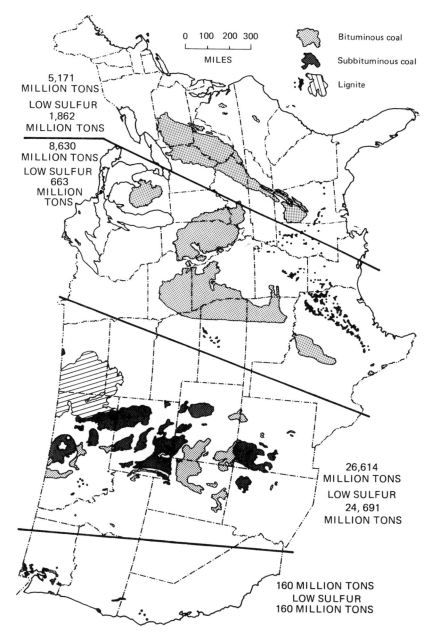

6.1. Strippable Reserves of the Conterminous United States, by Region. *Source: Reprinted from Strippable Reserves of Bituminous Coal and Lignite in the United States,* U.S. Dept. of Interior Bureau of Mines Info. Circ. 8531, Washington, D.C., 1971, p. 19.

Harmful conflict between oceanic oil transport and marine fisheries will materialize only if a number of factors, such as the occurrence of an oil spill, the sensitivity of its location, the season, and the wind direction, coincide to harm marine biota.

However, oil imports may also be a factor in more immediate conflicts of resource use. Foreign oil will require increased U.S. exports — including agricultural commodities such as wheat and soybeans — to maintain a favorable balance of trade. However, the U.S. capacity to produce food commodities could be threatened by the rising demand for another source of energy — coal. Much coal available for strip mining underlies lands which now grow wheat or other crops. (See maps, Figures 6.1 and 6.2.)

Wheat Versus Coal

Serious study is needed as to whether strip mining threatens the capacity of the United States to grow food, particularly if the nation sees its role as supplying food to needy countries. The conflict reveals yet another reason why a technology of energy conservation is necessary. In this case, energy conservation could postpone the necessity to strip mine coal beneath fertile agricultural lands.

In the United States, every state, including prime agricultural and wheat-growing states, has experienced surface mining of some sort.[15] As of 1972, 4 million acres of land had been disturbed by surface mining. Of that land formerly used for agriculture, more than half was unreclaimed.[16]

Moreover, the meaning of "reclaimed" is obscure. Evidence that agricultural lands in the United States can be restored to their former productivity on a large scale is elusive. On a small scale, test plots have indicated that forage crops could be grown on pasture land that had been mined and reclaimed.[17] In West Germany, methods have been developed to strip mine brown coal deposits and return the land to agricultural production.[18] At the Nikopol open-pit manganese mines in the Ukraine, the rich topsoil was carefully removed and then replaced after mining. After three to four years, orchards and grains were planted with apparent success.[19]

In this country "reclaimed" does not mean that strip mined lands have been returned to former uses. It means only that those lands have been adapted to some form of beneficial use. In northeastern Illinois, for example, farms once mined have not been restored to farms. Instead, the washboard terrain, interspersed with winding lakes, has become an outdoor recreation area for metropolitan Chicago.

Impediments to complete reclamation of strip mined lands are both physical and economic. The ability to reproduce a soil capable of supporting agricultural crops depends on soil composition, topography, and climate.[20] The thin fragile topsoils of semiarid regions in the West cannot be regenerated without adequate water supplies, which are already limited and may be exhausted by gasification or other processing of strip mined coal.[21]

Even if deeper Midwest soils can be returned to agricultural production, experiences in Britain[22] and West Germany[23] indicate that reclamation costs will

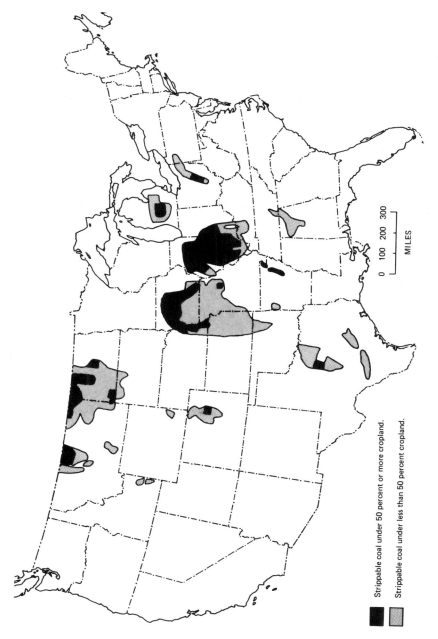

6.2. Cropland Overlying Coal. *Source*: "Commercial Wheat Production," U.S.D.A. Economic Research Service. Publ. No. 480 (1971); *Strippable Reserves of Bituminous Coal and Lignite*, p. 19.

reach $4,000 to $5,000 an acre. These costs could be expected to impede complete land reclamation in a nation such as the United States which until just recently had food surpluses and relatively cheap agricultural lands.

In the nation, more than 150,000 acres are newly disturbed by surface mining or related activities each year. As of 1973, surface mining for coal was expected to expand because of increasing demands for electrical power and increased costs of deep mining operations.

Strip mining is not the only threat posed to croplands. The U.S. Department of Agriculture estimated in 1971 that about 2 million acres of croplands a year in the United States are converted to nonagricultural uses.[24] Urban development takes 420,000 acres a year, airports and highways 160,000, reservoirs and flood control measures 420,000, and a million acres a year goes for parks, recreation areas, and wildlife refuges.[25]

"Though our land resources appear adequate to provide ample food supply for many years to come," the USDA said, "certain developments would alter the outlook." The USDA conclusion, which referred to the United States only, did not consider in 1971 the expanding importance of U.S. wheat in world trade. Wheat now has superseded rice as the world's predominant foodstuff.

If increased output were necessary, there would be two ways to expand agricultural production: increase the yield per acre or farm more land. According to the USDA, past increases in per-acre yields were achieved by a number of factors including improved varieties, higher use of fertilizer and pesticides, the elimination of less productive land from cropping, and land improvement practices such as drainage and irrigation.

"The economists do not have at hand the information necessary to assign to each of these factors its contribution to the overall growth in output," says USDA. "However, this much is evident: Future per-acre production gains of . . . 2 percent a year would depend to a considerable degree on continuing increases in uses of farm chemicals on land. If it becomes necessary to curtail usage of chemicals, per-acre yields would be less, and more land would be required to achieve a given level of production."[26]

Where Do Wheat and Coal Conflict?

Wheat farming is widely dispersed across the United States, but the heavy concentrations are in the Plains States and the Pacific Northwest. Wheat is a competitive crop not only under semiarid conditions in the West, but it competes with corn and other crops further east.[27] The Midwestern Corn Belt, an extremely fertile agricultural area, also grows a substantial amount of wheat.[28] (See maps, Figure 6.3.)

Large areas of primary wheat land — where wheat is at least 30 percent of planted crop acreage, and in most cases is at least 45 percent[29] — overlie strippable beds of bituminous, sub-bituminous and lignite coal in north central, northeastern, and parts of southern Montana.[30] (See map, Figure 6.1.) These reserves are predominantly low sulfur.[31] Large areas of primary wheat land also lie over

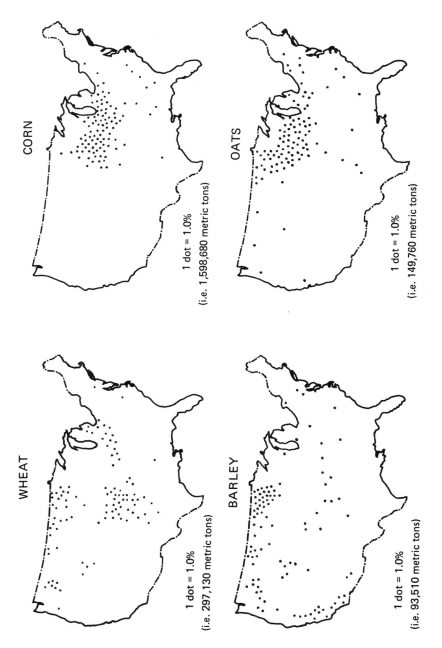

6.3.   Major Areas of Production for Selected United States Crops, 1962.
Source: *World Atlas of Agriculture, Vol. III, Americas*, Committee for the
World Atlas of Agriculture, Novara, Italy (1969) p. 453.

strippable lignite in western North Dakota and northwestern South Dakota. Secondary wheat lands — less than 30 percent of planted crop acreage — overlie strippable coal in eastern Nebraska, eastern Kansas, north central Missouri, central lower Michigan, and southwest and south central Illinois.[32]

Two of the wheat-over-coal states, Montana and Illinois, are already encountering significant conflicts in land use. Two other states, Iowa and North Dakota, contain large areas where strip mining may compete with crop production.

Montana.   Forty percent of the nation's reserves of low sulfur coal and lignite is under Montana, North Dakota, and Wyoming.[33] By the time the deposits are exhausted, about 800,000 acres of Montana alone could be stripped.[34] While Montana produced 1 million tons of low sulfur coal and lignite in 1969 (only 35,000 tons from underground mines),[35] the demand for low sulfur coal had increased production sevenfold by 1971,[36] two years later. Production of Montana coal continued to increase in 1972, though at a slower rate.[37] Strip mining activity could be further accelerated to 16 million tons in 1973, 20 million tons in 1975, and 75 to 80 million tons in 1980, according to a 1973 report by the Montana Coal Task Force.[38]

The Montana coal lies under the primarily agricultural eastern part of the state.[39] Eighty-five percent of the land is cropland, pasture, or range.[40] Part of the coal lies under a piece of the Northern Plains spring wheat region, one of the country's prime wheat production areas, according to the U.S. Geological Survey.[41] Montana is second in the nation in spring wheat acreage and third in production of winter and spring wheat.[42]

Noting that "current trends and forces make it clear that the state must and will have a central role in any system of land use planning,"[43] the Montana Coal Task Force in their January 1973 report explored the broad environmental, social, and economic impacts that coal development held in store for eastern Montana. The Task Force recommended the Montana Reclamation Act, which was passed by the state legislature in May 1973.[44] Among other provisions, the law required that strip mined land be restored to agricultural use. The state retained the right to refuse or revoke strip mining permits on environmental grounds.

Illinois.   Illinois is one of the largest and oldest coal producing areas in the United States.[45] In 1971, it produced 58 million tons of coal, ranking fourth in national production. Furthermore, it led the nation in coal reserves with an estimated 19 billion tons. About half of the state's production comes from strip mining,[46] and in 1967 Illinois led the nation in strip coal production.[47] Most Illinois coal is high in sulfur content.[48] The eastern interior coal field, which underlies the southern three-quarters of Illinois, southwestern Indiana, and northwestern Kentucky, is shaped like an elongated saucer. Mining is carried out mostly toward the edges where seams are nearer the surface. Coal quality improves toward the south of the field.[49]

Although the two major grain crops for Illinois are corn and soybeans, the state is high in wheat production, ranking seventh nationally in the production of winter

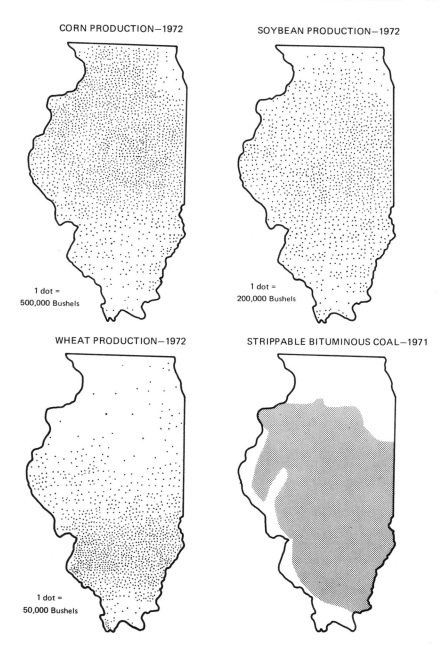

6.4. Croplands and Strippable Coal Lands in Illinois. *Sources*: *Illinois Agricultural Statistics, 1973 Summary*, Ill. Crop Rept. Ser. Bul. 73-1, Springfield, 1973, p. 12; *Strippable Reserves of Bituminous Coal and Lignite*, p. 19.

wheat.[50] Some of the state's better wheat lands, as well as highly productive corn and soybean croplands, lie over strippable coal reserves (see maps, Figure 6.4).

Yet, in spite of the growing need for coal and increasing need for crops, there was in Illinois in 1973 a general feeling that the state had abundant croplands.

"Right now land for our two major grain crops . . . is abundant enough that the more philosophical questions of weighing alternative land uses have not been acted upon," said Neal Gunkel, assistant to the director of the Illinois Department of Agriculture in 1973.[51] "They will come to the front in the next five years as agricultural production becomes even more important."

In a 1973 Environmental Impact Statement prepared for the proposed nuclear station in LaSalle County, Illinois, the Atomic Energy Commission staff observed:

> The present agricultural activities are being carried on for economic reasons. The staff concludes that the specific agricultural activities at the site are unnecessary to the general population for the next 40 to 50 years; that these activities have been and continue to be highly disruptive to the natural environment . . . and are being carried on for the principal benefit of the families owning and or residing on the land, since an oversupply of the commodity produced on the land is projected for the next 40 to 50 years.[52]

During 1972, about 7,000 acres of land in Illinois were newly affected by strip mining. About 4,200 acres of that were cropland, 1,500 acres were forest, and 1,200 were pasture.[53]

Unanswered Questions about the Wheat and Coal Conflict

The scale of the potential conflict is elusive. Simple quantification of the acreages involved suggests that the conflict, if there is one, is relatively small. For example, Figure 6.5 shows that of the 2.3 billion acres of land in the fifty United States, 15 percent was used for crops in 1969, whereas mining of all kinds occupied less than three-tenths of 1 percent (0.3%). Furthermore, the 5-million-acre total expected to be disturbed from mining by 1980 would approach but 2 percent of the total cropland *if all the mining occurred on cropland.*

However, with the increasingly delicate balance of world food supplies[54] and the rising significance of foodstuffs as export commodities for the United States, a number of unpredictable variables could affect the picture immensely. One could be a greater reliance upon coal than foreseen, if nuclear electrical generating capacity failed to come on line as predicted, or if a means were developed to remove sulfur from coal either at the coal fields or at generating plants.

Another variable is the relative productivity of land lying over coal fields. Some of the world's most productive land and most favorable climatic conditions occur in the Midwest. Both Iowa and Illinois which fall within this region are underlain with vast strippable coal reserves, estimated by some investigators to include half of Iowa and 40 percent of Illinois.[55] The loss of one acre of average Illinois farmland may have many times the impact on total protein production as the loss of a single acre of Montana or North Dakota cropland. A complicating factor is the current

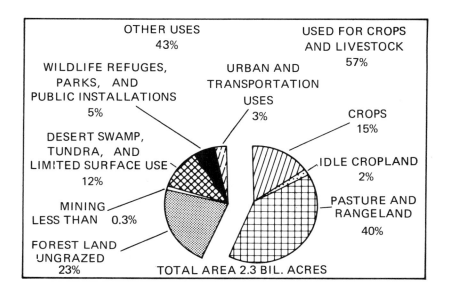

6.5.   Land Use in the United States, 1969. *Source: Material Needs & The Environment*, National Commission on Materials Policy, 1973.

uncertainty as to whether there are economically feasible methods for rapidly restoring land to its former productivity on a large scale. Nowhere is there evidence that *complete* restoration has been achieved on a large scale anywhere in the United States.

Another unknown is the extent of future increase in per-acre productivity, not only in the United States but in the rest of the world, through new techniques, new strains of grain, and new fertilizers. Furthermore, national decisions in the United States and other nations, such as the Soviet Union or Japan, on whether to encourage beef or other protein-concentrating industries, will determine how much grain is needed to satisfy human consumption. (It takes about five times as much grain to produce animal protein as it does to satisfy man's protein needs by direct consumption of grain.)[56]

An additional important question is how the coal is to be extracted — by underground mining or by strip mining. Production in the bituminous coal industry, which is based mainly in the Midwest and Appalachia, has been remarkably consistent for half a century. In 1920, 569 million tons of bituminous were produced. In 1971, 552 million tons were produced. In the record year, 1947, 631 million tons were mined; the low year, 1932, produced 310 million tons.[57] With automation, 704,000 employees in 1923 dropped to 140,000 employees in 1971.[58] Even more dramatic than automation was the shift to strip mining. In 1920, 1.5 percent of the total production was strip mined. By 1971, 46.9 percent was strip mined.[59] The later years reported were those of greatest growth. Rapid growth in strip mining can be expected to continue indefinitely.

Looking Beyond the Dilemma

While the world seems to be moving away from a position of having adequate if not surplus food production, new threats are posed to terrestrial and aquatic sources of food by the increasing demand for energy. Forums within which these conflicts might be resolved comprehensively do not exist or are not being used. The issues are being decided on a piecemeal basis at the local level.

This dilemma re-emphasizes the need for national long-range policy on natural resources. It is critical that public and private resource decision-makers be forced, as a matter of policy, to look beyond immediate problems to the consequences that lie ahead. Until all aspects of a problem are considered and all available knowledge is used, regrettable decisions will continue to be made.

But while we wait for America to awaken to the need for long-range resource planning, we can at least encourage a technology of energy conservation that may alleviate some conflicts in resource use and perhaps even obviate others. Like the "Faustian bargains" in Chapter 5, the food versus fuel conflict offers another reason for vigorously pursuing the conservation of materials and energy.

References

1. Lester R. Brown, "The World Gets Hungrier and U.S. Abundance Dwindles," *Milwaukee Journal*, August 19, 1973; Communication to Leonardo Seminar, May 2, 1973, by members of the Canadian Wheat Board.
2. See the discussion in Chapter 1, above, pp. 7-8.
3. *Bituminous Coal Facts, 1972,* National Coal Association, (Washington, D.C.: 1972), p. 8.
4. U.S., Congress, House, Committee on Interior and Insular Affairs, "Fuel and Energy Resources, 1972," Part II: Hearings, 92nd Congress, 2nd session, April 14, 17-19, 1972. Statement by Joseph P. Brennan, p. 926, Table 1.
5. As defined by the United States Geological Survey, low sulfur coal contains less than 1 percent sulfur, medium sulfur coal contains 1 to 3 percent sulfur and high sulfur coal has more than 3 percent sulfur. (D. A. Brobst and W. B. Pratt, eds., *United States Mineral Resources*, USGS Paper 820 [Washington, D.C.: U.S. Government Printing Office, 1973], p. 135.
6. Brobst and Pratt, *U.S. Mineral Resources*, p. 135.
7. Roger Revelle, Edward Wenk, Bostwick H. Ketchum, and Edward R. Corino, "Ocean Pollution by Petroleum Hydrocarbons," in William H. Matthews, ed., *Man's Impact on Terrestrial and Oceanic Ecosystems*, (Cambridge, Mass.: MIT Press 1971), pp. 300-02.
8. Douglas L. Inman and Birchard M. Brush, "The Coastal Challenge," *Science* 181:27 (July 6, 1973).
9. "Deepwater Ports: Issue Mixes Supertankers, Land Policy," *Science* 181:825 (August 31, 1973).
10. Ibid.
11. Revelle et al., "Ocean Pollution by Petroleum Hydrocarbons," p. 299.
12. Revelle et al., "Ocean Pollution by Petroleum Hydrocarbons," p. 297; also Max Blumer, "Scientific Aspects of the Oil Spill Problem," *Environmental Affairs*, vol. 1, no. 1, 55 (April 1972)

13. Bostwick H. Ketchum, "Biological Implications of Global Marine Pollution," in S. Fred Singer, ed., *Global Effects of Environmental Pollution* (New York: Springer-Verlag, 1970), p. 194; Wesley Marx, *Oilspill* (San Francisco: Sierra Club, 1971), pp. 28, 51-52.

14. William Longgood, *The Darkening Land* (New York: Simon and Schuster, 1972), p. 40.

15. U.S.,Congress, Senate, Committee on Interior and Insular Affairs, *Surface Mining Reclamation*: Hearings on S.3132, S.3126, and S.217, 90th Congress, 2nd session, April 30-May 2, 1968, p. 37.

16. *Coal Surface Mining and Reclamation: An Environmental and Economic Assessment of Alternatives*, Report of the Council on Environmental Quality (Washington, D.C.: U.S. Government Printing Office, 1973), p. 1.

17. U.S., Congress, Senate, Committee on Interior and Insular Affairs, *Problems of Electical Power Production in the Southwest, Part I:* Hearings, 92nd Congress, 1st session, May 24, 1971, pp. 220-21, 227-30.

18. E. A. Nephew, "Healing Wounds," *Environment*, January-February 1972, pp. 17-20.

19. Brobst and Pratt, *U.S. Mineral Resources, p. 387.*

20. Restoring Surface Mined Land, U.S. Department of Agriculture, Miscellaneous Publication No. 1082 (Washington, D.C.: 1968), pp. 5-6.

21. "NAS: Water Scarcity May Limit Use of Western Coals," *Science* 181:525 (August 10, 1973); Sally Jacobsen, "The Great Montana Coal Rush," *Science and Public Affairs*, April 1973, pp. 39-40.

22. Harry M. Caudill, "Farming and Mining," *Atlantic*, September 1973, pp. 89-90.

23. Nephew, "Healing Wounds," pp. 14-15.

24. "Agriculture in the Environment," *The Farm Index*, March-June 1971, reprinted in U.S. Department of Agriculture, Economics Research Service Bulletin. ERS 481, July 1971, p. 7.

25. Agricultural lands converted to parks and recreational uses do not necessarily lose their capacity for reconversion later. However, urban development, airports, highways, and reservoirs have the same impact on agricultural land as strip mining insofar as extensive restoration is required before the land can be used for crops again.

26. "Agriculture in the Environment," p. 7.

27. *Commercial Wheat Production*, U.S. Department of Agriculture, Economics Research Service Bulletin, ERS 480, September 1971, p. 6.

28. Ibid., p. 3.

29. Ibid., p. 5.

30. *Strippable Reserves of Bituminous Coal and Lignite in the United State*, U.S. Department of Interior, Bureau of Mines Information Circular 8531, 1971, p. 19.

31. Ibid., p. 96.

32. Ibid., p. 19; *Commercial Wheat Production,* p. 5.

33. "Showdown in Montana," *Time*, April 16, 1973, p. 62.

34. *Coal Development in Eastern Montana*, Department of Natural Resources and Conservation (Helena, Mont.: 1973), p. 62.

35. *1969 Minerals Yearbook*, U.S. Department of Interior, Bureau of Mines, Vol. I-II, pp. 318-20.

36. *Bituminous Coal Facts, 1972*, p. 56.

37. "Mineral Industry Surveys," U.S. Department of Interior, Bureau of Mines, Weekly Coal Report 2902, April 27, 1973.

38. *Coal Development*, p. 14.

39. Ibid., p. 62.

40. Ibid.
41. *The National Atlas of the United States of America*, U.S. Department of Interior, Geological Survey (Washington, D.C.: 1970), map, p. 170.
42. U.S. Department of Agriculture, *Agricultural Statistics, 1972* (Washington, D.C.: U.S. Government Printing Office, 1972), Table 3, p. 5.
43. *Coal Development*, p. 72.
44. Ibid.
45. *Strippable Reserves of Bituminous Coal*, p. 34.
46. *1969 Minerals Yearbook*, Vol. I-II, pp. 318-20.
47. *Strippable Reserves of Bituminous Coal*, p. 34.
48. Ibid.
49. Reed Moyer, *Competition in the Midwest Coal Industry*, (Cambridge, Mass.: Harvard University Press, 1964), pp. 12-13.
50. *Agricultural Statistics 1972*, Table 3, p. 4.
51. Personal communication to the Leonardo Seminar.
52. Commonwealth Edison Co., "Final Environmental Statement Related to the Lasalle County Nuclear Station," U.S. Atomic Energy Commission, 1973, p. xii-11.
53. Personal communication from Ross Richardson, administrative assistant, Illinois Department of Mines and Minerals, 1973.
54. See discussion above in this chapter; see also "World Food Situation: Pessimism Comes Back Into Vogue," *Science* 181:634-38 (August 17, 1973).
55. Caudill, "Farming and Mining," p. 88.
56. Louis M. Thompson, "The World Food Situation," *Journal of Soil and Water Conservation*, January–February 1972, p. 4.
57. *Bituminous Coal Facts, 1972*, pp. 52-53.
58. Ibid.
59. Ibid.

7.   Conservation of Materials and Energy

The wise resolution of a "Faustian bargain" or of a conflict between uses of different but equally needed resources requires careful policy decisions. Rapidly growing demands for energy and materials may force such decisions sooner than expected. The coal versus wheat conflict and the question of nuclear power plant waste disposal both are with us in some small degree, yet their solutions are not. Without ready solutions, the best course may be to slow down the rush into unknown areas. Postponement allows time to carefully weigh the far-reaching consequences of final commitments. It allows time to solve technical problems of nuclear waste disposal and strip mine reclamation or to find totally new solutions. At present, only one alternative will allow us to postpone such decisions — that is, to conscientiously conserve materials and energy on a national scale.

The notion of conservation is not yet popular, but it is a realistic way to "buy time." Much conserving can be done with no danger of returning to the "cave and candles era" envisioned by critics of conservation. Indeed, this chapter suggests ways for achieving enormous savings without significant changes in lifestyle.

Energy and Materials Flow

Before considering conservation measures, it is useful to understand how energy and materials flow through both the natural environment and the human enterprise, and how the processing of materials affects consumption of energy.

Physical scientists approach the concepts of resource "use" and "waste" not in terms of commodities "produced" and "consumed," but rather as natural resources that are *transformed* into objects of value or service to people. Transformation also creates incidental products which have no immediate value or may be harmful. Economists refer to these by-products as *residuals*.[1] When the residuals can be identified as having some harmful effect, they are called *pollutants*.[2] Examples are the SO_2 gas and the trace amounts of lead and arsenic emitted by the combustion of coal.

Every process that transforms or moves a material requires energy. Energy is required when ore is taken from the ground, when ore is smelted and refined into metal, and when the metal is made into brass jewelry or transistors. Energy is required when wheat is made into bread. Even the release of energy stored in fuels like oil and coal requires other energy to extract, concentrate, transport, and convert the fuel to usable forms. *Transformation technology* refers to the use of energy to convert natural resources into commodities and residuals.

The flows and interactions of materials and energy can be traced by means of diagrams. Figure 7.1 shows general flows of terrestrial materials and energy

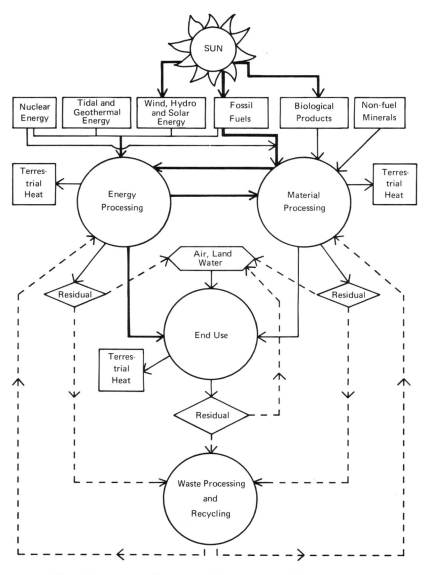

7.1.   Flow Diagram for Terrestrial Materials and Energy.

through the human enterprise. By the familiar laws of physics that matter and energy are neither created nor destroyed, the end products of resource processing — that is, the commodity and its residuals — must equal the matter and energy that went into the processing. However, there is a fundamental difference between the flow of energy and the flow of materials. While material residuals and commodities often can be gathered from their dispersed locations and reconcentrated, the energy spent in processing dissipates and can never be gathered together again.

As energy is used, it degrades from an orderly, high-energy state to a less orderly, lower state. The degree of disorder associated with the energy is called *entropy*. Energy always must flow in such a direction that entropy or disorder increases. The various forms of energy thus can be classified in an "order of merit," the highest form being the one with the least entropy. For example, the energy of a burning light bulb moves from high quality radiant energy to lower quality heat energy, or *waste energy*, which is a common residual of material transformations.

While generally useless to man because of its dissipated nature, waste energy still may be abundant enough to become a pollutant. In 1972, 12.5 quadrillion (or 12.5 x 10^{15}) BTUs[3] of low quality heat were rejected as waste from electric power plants in the United States. Insofar as the residual heat was not used in some other way, such as heating fish hatchery ponds or commercial buildings, it was wasted. Insofar as it entered and degraded valued aquatic systems, it was a pollutant.

In a sense, the flow of energy through the human enterprise is a "once-through" system. There can be no recycling of energy. It can, however, be conserved and its use can be extended by more efficient transformations.

How much energy and materials are we using now and, more importantly, how much of that could be saved? In 1972 the total energy flowing through the human enterprise in the United States was 72.1 quadrillion BTUs.[4] Such large, unwieldy numbers have caused scientists to devise new energy units. The largest of these is the "Q" unit, which is 1,000,000,000,000,000,000 (10^{18}) BTUs. The Q has been roughly calculated as the amount of energy necessary to raise the water temperature in Lake Ontario from the freezing point to the boiling point and is sometimes referred to as "Ontario."

In 1972 the United States used .072 Q. The overall efficiency of this energy system as it flowed from sources, through conversions of energy, to production of commodities and residuals, was 50 percent (see Figure 7.2). The other 50 percent of energy that entered the flow spun off as residual before it reached the ultimate U.S. energy users, called *end users*. In 1968, the end users fell into four broad categories: 20 percent were homes; 14 percent, commercial enterprises; 41 percent, industry; and 25 percent, transportation.

In 1972 the U.S. energy flow was accompanied by a materials flow of 4.4 billion tons, or 42,500 pounds per American, excluding food (Figure 7.3). If food had been included in the flow, it would have increased the weight for each American by about 10 percent, or another 4,000 pounds.

Figure 7.1 suggests that much of the one-way flow of materials can be stopped. Waste reprocessing and recycling offer many opportunities to close the materials loop; and, as will be seen, reusing materials also results in energy conservation. While there is no way to stop the flow of usable energy out of the human enterprise,

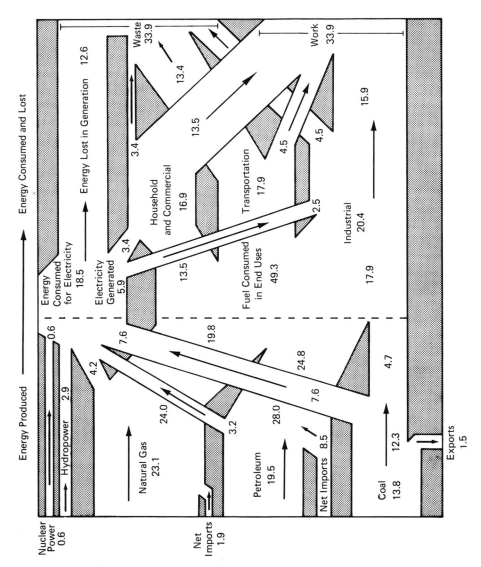

7.2. Flow of Energy Through the U.S. System in 1972 (in quadrillion BTUs). Total consumption of energy in 1972 was 67.9 quadrillion BTU. The nonenergy use of fuels, primarily for petrochemicals, raised the total to 72.0 quadrillion BTU. Overall efficiency of the system was 50 percent. The efficiency of electrical generation and transmission was estimated at 32 percent. Efficiency of direct fuel use in transportation was about 25 percent. Efficiency in other non-electrical use of energy was estimated at 75 percent and efficiency for end use of electricity at 100 percent. Hydropower was assumed to be generated with an energy use of 10,494 BTU /kwhr. *Source:* Re-drawn from "The Flow of Energy in An Industrial Society" by Earl Cook. Copyright September 1971 by Scientific American, Inc. 1972 figures based on U.S. Department of Interior data.

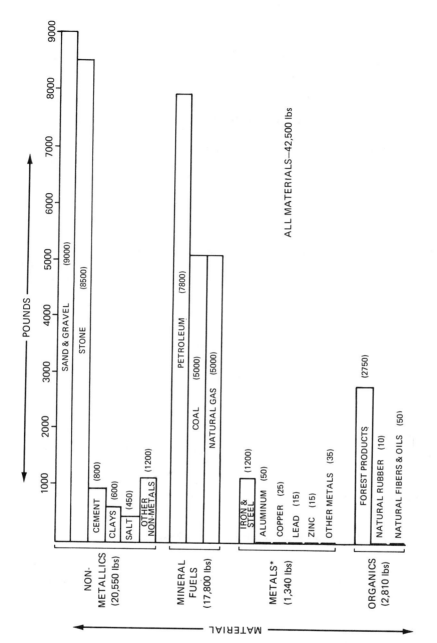

7.3. Weight of Raw Materials Required Per Capita in the U.S. in 1972. The amount of new basic mineral and non-food organic materials used by the average U.S. citizen in 1972 totaled 42,500 lbs. *Source: Material Needs and the Environment Today and Tomorrow,* Final Report of the National Communion on Materials Policy, 1973.

the flow can be slowed by materials conservation, more efficient use of available energy, and a change in production and consumption patterns.

Opportunities for Energy Conservation

Where in the energy flow diagram are the opportunities for conservation? A rich developing literature suggests that at almost every point, from extraction of raw fuels to final use of energy in home and factory, there are many ways to reduce energy flow.

An early study by the Federal Office of Emergency Preparedness[5] speculated that vigorous conservation measures could reduce the estimated energy demand for the year 1980 by the energy equivalent of over 7 million barrels of oil per day. (Energy equivalent refers here to that amount of oil which would contain the same number of BTUs as all fuels consumed in 1980.) This is an impressive figure when compared with projected daily imports for 1980 of over 10 million barrels per day. The report concluded that the most significant and practical measures to effect conservation are

> 1. improved insulation in homes,
> 2. adoption of more efficient air-conditioning systems,
> 3. shift of intercity freight from highway to rail and shift of intercity passengers from air to ground travel and urban passengers from automobile to mass transit, and
> 4. introduction of more efficient industrial processes and equipment.

Additional studies at Oak Ridge National Laboratory, at the National Bureau of Standards, and at other research centers have confirmed the potential of most of these measures.[6]

The remainder of this section will take a closer look at two of these general areas: improvements in home insulation systems and changes in transportation systems.

Improved Space Heating and Cooling Practices

Building design has an extraordinary influence on the use of energy, particularly heat. The influence tends to be lasting as the occupant generally is bound to use patterns specified by designers and builders. As a result, architecture has an impact on total energy consumption exceeded only by transportation and, perhaps, the military. In the United States, space heating of private and commercial buildings is the second largest end use of energy, amounting to 20 percent of national energy consumption (Table 7.1). Of this amount, nonresidential users contribute 9 percent; the remaining 11 percent goes to residences. Space heating uses an average of over half the energy delivered to an all-electric home in a moderate climate. It uses an even higher fraction for nonelectrically heated homes. With a growth rate close to that for all energy, space heating is clearly a field that could benefit from energy conservation measures.

TABLE 7.1. Energy Consumption in the United States by End Use 1960–1968 (Trillions of BTU and percent per year)

Sector and End Use	Consumption 1960	Consumption 1968	Annual Rate of Growth	Percent of National Total 1960	Percent of National Total 1968
Residential					
Space heating	4,848	6,675	4.1%	11.3%	11.0%
Water heating	1,159	1,736	5.2	2.7	2.9
Cooking	556	637	1.7	1.3	1.1
Clothes drying	93	208	10.6	0.2	0.3
Refrigeration	369	692	8.2	0.9	1.1
Air conditioning	134	427	15.6	0.3	0.7
Other	809	1,241	5.5	1.9	2.1
Total	7,968	11,616	4.8	18.6	19.2
Commercial					
Space heating	3,111	4,182	3.8	7.2	6.9
Water heating	544	653	2.3	1.3	1.1
Cooking	98	139	4.5	0.2	0.2
Refrigeration	534	670	2.9	1.2	1.1
Air conditioning	576	1,113	8.6	1.3	1.8
Feedstock	734	984	3.7	1.7	1.6
Other	145	1,025	28.0	0.3	1.7
Total	5,742	8,766	5.4	13.2	14.4
Industrial					
Process steam	7,646	10,132	3.6	17.8	16.7
Electric drive	3,170	4,794	5.3	7.4	7.9
Electrolytic processes	486	705	4.8	1.1	1.2
Direct heat	5,550	6,929	2.8	12.9	11.5
Feed stock	1,370	2,202	6.1	3.2	3.6
Other	118	198	6.7	0.3	0.3
Total	18,340	24,960	3.9	42.7	41.2
Transportation					
Fuel	10,873	15,038	4.1	25.2	24.9
Raw materials	141	146	0.4	0.3	0.3
Total	11,014	15,184	4.1	25.5	25.2
National total	43,064	60,526	4.3	100.0%	100.0%

Note: Electric utility consumption has been allocated to each end use.
Source: Stanford Research Institute, using Bureau of Mines and other sources.

Improved insulation is the most promising approach. The National Bureau of Standards has stated that better insulation and construction processes could cut by 40 to 50 percent the nation's total residential and commercial space heating and cooling requirements in both old and new structures.[7] An important step was taken in 1971 with passage of the Federal Housing Administration's significantly tightened insulation requirements for single family dwellings.[8]

Potential energy conservation and financial savings from improved insulation have been evaluated by Eric Hirst and John Moyers[9,10] of Oak Ridge National Laboratory. Moyers and Hirst estimated the heating requirements under various insulation conditions for typical homes in three climates of the United States — Atlanta, New York, and Minneapolis. Table 7.2 presents monetary and energy savings that resulted when a New York residence was insulated according to both the unrevised and revised FHA minimum property standards (MPS).

The net savings in dollars from insulation are realized annually over the life of the home and begin after installation costs are recovered. For a gas-heated home, the revised minimum property standards save $28 annually and reduce energy consumption by 29 percent a year. For an electrically heated home the corresponding figures are $5 and 19 percent. This difference is due to two factors: insulation standards for electrically heated homes are already higher than the requirements for gas-heated homes; and electric heat is more expensive than gas. Hirst and Moyers found that to achieve the "economic optimum" insulation, that is, the insulation thickness providing maximum monetary savings to the home owner, it was necessary to exceed FHA standards. The savings for a gas-heated home with optimum insulation are $32 and 49 percent respectively, and for an electrically heated home, $155 and 47 percent.

Such savings would have a tremendous impact upon domestic energy requirements. Hirst and Moyers point out that

> An average savings of 42 percent, applied to the space heating energy requirements for all residential units (single family and apartment, gas and electric) would have amounted to 3,100 trillion BTU in 1970.[11]

This is 4.6 percent of total energy consumption in the United States, or *two and one-half times more than the total energy used for all purposes in the state of Wisconsin in 1970.*[12] Moreover, even these massive energy savings may be conservative since heat from lights, stoves, and other utilities contribute significantly to home heating as insulation is added. Air-conditioning requirements also would be reduced as insulation keeps the cool air in and the hot air out.

Other opportunities exist for energy conservation in homes through the use of electrical heat pumps, high efficiency air conditioners, gas appliances without pilot lights, and low energy construction materials.

Improved Transportation Systems

Transportation of people and goods consumed about 17.9 quadrillion BTU, or 25 percent of total energy used in the United States in 1972 (Figure 7.2). Most forecasters expect this fraction to remain reasonably constant as total energy usage grows. Past increases in transportation energy demand were due mainly to increased

TABLE 7.2. Monetary Savings and Reduction of Energy Consumption for a New York Residence Under Various Insulation Conditions

Insulation Specifications	Unrevised FHA Minimum Property Standards*		Revised FHA Minimum Property Standards*		Insulation Providing Economic Optimum for Homeowner	
	Gas Heating	Electric Heating	Gas Heating	Electric Heating	Gas Heating	Electric Heating
Thickness of wall insulation (inches)	0	1-7/8	1-7/8	1-7/8	3-1/2	3-1/2
Thickness of ceiling insulation (inches)	1-7/8	1-7/8	3-1/2	3-1/2	3-1/2	6
Floor insulation	No	No	Yes	Yes	Yes	Yes
Storm windows	No	No	No	No	Yes	Yes
Monetary savings ($/yr.)	0	0	28	75	32	155
Reduction of energy consumption (%)	0	0	29	19	49	47

*Minimum Property Standards for one and two living units.

Source: Eric Hirst and John C. Moyers, "Efficiency of Energy Use in the United States."

TABLE 7.3.   Energy Intensiveness of Freight and Passenger Transport

Passenger Mode	Actual Load Factor (%)[1]	BTU/Passenger-mile (Actual Load Factor)	BTU/Passenger-mile (100% Load Factor)
Walking[2]	100	300	—
Bicycle[2]	100	180	—
Urban auto[3]	28	8,100	2,300
Urban mass transit[3]	20	3,800	760
Inter-city auto[3]	48	3,400	1,600
Inter-city bus[3]	46	1,600	740
Rail[3]	37	2,900	1,100
Airplane[3]	39	8,400	4,100
Freight Mode		BTU/Ton-mile	
Rail[4]		670	
Water[4]		680	
Truck[4]		2,800	
Airplane[4]		42,000	

[1]The load factor is the number of passengers present as a percentage of total passenger capacity. The actual load factor is the national average of passenger loading, computed from available data as discussed on pp. 27–28 and the appendix to *Energy Intensiveness,* footnote 3 below. Assuming miles/gallon remain constant as the number of passengers increases, energy intensiveness declines as more passengers are carried per vehicle.

[2]Source: Eric Hirst, *Energy Consumption for Transportation in the U.S.,* Oak Ridge National Laboratory Report NSF-EP-15, 1972, Table 7, p. 13. The energy expenditure is human energy.

[3]Source: Eric Hirst, *Energy Intensiveness of Passenger and Freight Transport Modes, 1950–1970,* Oak Ridge National Laboratory Report NSF-EP-44, 1973, Table 12, p. 27.

[4]Source: Ibid., Table 11, p. 27. Assumptions and data sources are given in the appendix.

traffic measured as passenger-miles or ton-miles of freight, and shifts toward less efficient methods of transportation. In transportation, energy efficiency is defined in passenger-miles/BTU or ton-miles/BTU for freight. The inverse of this, energy intensiveness, is expressed in BTU/mile. Energy intensiveness of various transport modes is shown in Table 7.3. It is important to note that mile varies according to the load factor, that is the number of passengers actually present as a percentage of the total passenger capacity of the vehicle.

Energy consumed by nationwide intercity passenger transport grew by 170 percent between 1950 and 1970. This increase resulted from a 130 percent increase in traffic volume between cities and a 14 percent decrease in energy efficiency of passenger transport in the last decade.[13] The latter figure can be attributed to increased air travel, declining use of railroads and buses, and more powerful, less efficient autos. As shown in Table 7.3, the airplane is much less efficient in energy use than the train, the bus, or even the auto.

Between 1950 and 1970 significant increases occurred in urban passenger-miles as more people moved about within the city. This growth was accompanied by a 166 percent increase in energy consumption in urban transport.[14] However, because mass transit declined during this period, much of the increased energy use was also attributable to declines in energy efficiency. For example, Wisconsin urban bus systems (Figure 7.5) experienced a sharp decrease in miles traveled from 1950 to 1960, and a more gradual decrease from 1960 to the present.[15] It is clear that in our search for ever-increasing speed, power, and convenience, Americans have sacrificed overall energy efficiency in transportation.[16]

Like passenger transport, intercity freight transport also has grown rapidly in the past few decades. Between 1950 and 1970 energy consumption in this sector increased 102 percent. Most growth could be attributed to increased volumes of freight moved, but part of it was due to a 13 percent decline in energy efficiency, the result of shipping more goods by truck and plane and less by rail.

Shift to Smaller Passenger Vehicles

Disregarding for the moment the social problems of implementing changes in transport systems, let us investigate the potential savings in the use of more efficient transportation. The state of Wisconsin is a good example for such a study. In population, area, and automobiles per capita, Wisconsin is close to the national average. The increased energy demands of Wisconsin auto transport are shown in Figure 7.4. University of Wisconsin engineers, using a simulation model, (a

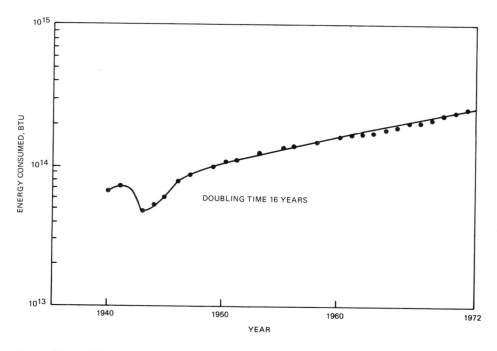

7.4. Total Motor Vehicle Energy Consumption in Wisconsin. *Source*: M. A. Caruso, "Energy Use for Transportation in Wisconsin: A Mathematical Model," M.S., 1973, University of Wisconsin-Madison.

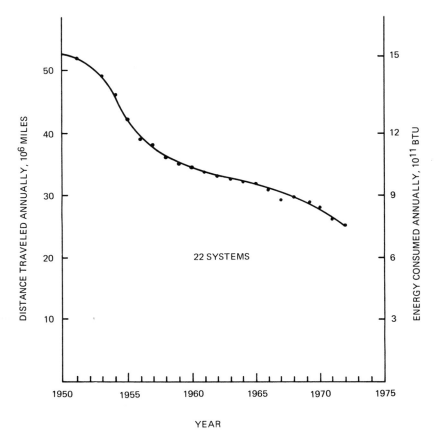

YEAR

7.5. Miles Traveled and Energy Consumed by Wisconsin Urban Bus Systems. *Source*: W. K. Foell, et at., "1973 Survey of Energy Use in Wisconsin" Report 10, Institute for Environmental Studies, University of Wisconsin-Madison.

simulation model is defined in Chapter 4, pp. 50-57), developed alternative "transportation futures" for Wisconsin. The model simulates energy used by both passenger and freight transport in the state, its regions, and its cities.[17]

In 1970, passenger automobiles consumed 63 percent of the total energy consumed by transportation. Would a shift to smaller autos with higher energy efficiencies result in substantial energy savings? To answer this question, the Wisconsin modeling team examined two possible futures for the state's vehicle population. In both cases, the passenger-miles traveled were assumed to be the same and two vehicle types were considered — conventional autos (weighing between 2,500 and 5,000 pounds) and small auto (weighing approximately 2,300 pounds). In "Future I," it was assumed that present conventional automobiles would continue in popularity. "Future II" assumed small autos would gradually replace conventional autos. A small drop in fuel economy, beginning in 1975 and leveling off in 1980, was calculated in anticipation of pollution control equipment to be added to all gasoline autos in 1976.

In "Future I" the assumption of constant vehicle preference led to increased energy use roughly proportional to increased demand for transport. The shift toward smaller, less energy-demanding autos in "Future II" kept energy use from growing significantly. Differences in energy consumption between the two futures was dramatic (Figure 7.6). In the year 2000, "Future II" shows annual savings of 435 million gallons of gasoline per year or 27 percent of the total used for passenger

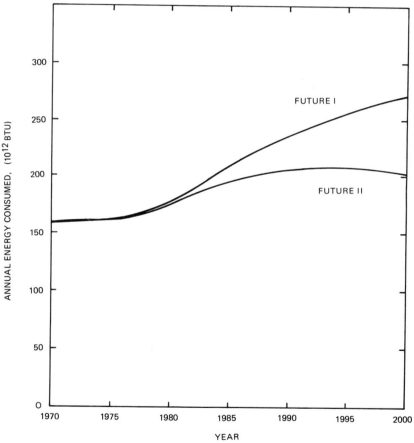

7.6. Two Energy Consumption Profiles for Passenger Auto Transport. Future I assumes continued consumer preference for large autos and continued increased demand for auto transport. Future II assumes a consumer shift to small, less energy demanding autos. *Source*: M. A. Caruso, "Energy Use for Transportation in Wisconsin: A Mathematical Model," M.S., 1973, University of Wisconsin-Madison.

vehicles in that year. Between 1970 and 2000, the accumulated savings amounted to 5.94 billion gallons, more than four and one-half times the quantity of gasoline used by all autos in Wisconsin in 1970. Not included is the energy saved indirectly through the use of less metal and other materials in the manufacture of smaller autos.

Shift to Energy-Efficient Freight Transport

A similar study was made on the impact of shifting freight transport to energy-efficient systems. It was assumed that regardless of transport mode, total freight movement would continue to increase in the future. "Future I" assumed a continuation of past trends, that is, a further shift away from rail to truck and planes. But "Future II" assumed a leveling off of the shift toward air freight and modest increases in rail freight (Table 7.4).

TABLE 7.4.   Distribution of Freight Transport in "Futures I and II"

Year	Future I (continuation of past trends) Percent of Total Ton-miles		
	Rail	Air	Truck
1970	69.3	.1	30.6
1975	69.2	.2	30.6
1980	69.2	.2	30.6
1985	69.2	.2	30.6
1990	69.1	.3	30.6
1995	69.1	.3	30.6
2000	69.0	.4	30.6
	Future II (shifts to more efficiency)		
1970	69.3	.1	30.6
1975	69.2	.2	30.6
1980	69.8	.2	30.0
1985	71.4	.2	28.4
1990	72.8	.2	27.0
1995	74.0	.2	25.8
2000	75.2	.2	24.6

Source: M. H. Caruso, "Energy Use for Transportation in Wisconsin: A Mathematical Model."

Both shifts in "Future II" lead to decreases in truck transport. The energy savings in "Future II" is clear in Figure 7.7. Annual savings in the year 2000 are 41 million gallons of gasoline. Cumulative savings between 1970 and 2000 amount to 460 million gallons.

The present mix of passenger and freight transport is determined by convenience, economics, speed, and public policy. Although problems of implementing trans-

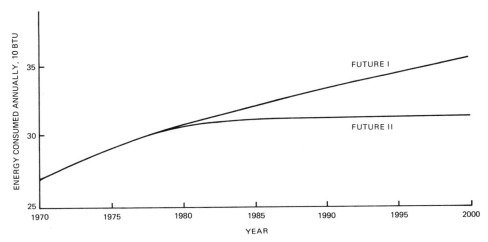

7.7.   Two Energy Consumption Profiles for Freight Transport. Future I
assumes a further shift away from rail transport and increased reliance on truck and
planes. Future II assumes a leveling off of air freight usage and modest increases in
rail freight. *Source*: M. A. Caruso, "Energy Use for Transportation in Wisconsin:
A Mathematical Model," M.S., 1973, University of Wisconsin-Madison.

portation conservation measures are significant — for example, financing the initial
costs of designing energy-efficient autos — *there seem to be no serious technological
barriers to proposed conservation practices*. The main barrier to energy conservation in all forms is a reluctance to commit human resources to the effort.

Recycling

Recycling, an approach to energy and material conservation introduced to the
American public with the "environmental awareness" of the late 1960s and early
1970s, brought a popular recognition of the need to "stop wasting," "stop
pollution," and "conserve natural resources." Concerned housewives began to
flatten used food cans, youth groups began to conduct paper drives, and "ecology
clubs" sprang up locally to pressure bottlers into restoring honor to the returnable
bottle system. Whether or not such early efforts could be justified in the prevailing
economic or resource picture, the citizen recyclers were correct from the point of
view of natural science. A growing economy based on wastage could not remain in
harmony with the natural environment.

The idea of recycling did not attract serious attention from government or private
research and study groups until the late 1960s. In 1969, the U.S. Senate Committee
on Public Works held hearings on the proposed Resource Recovery Act. The act,[18]
passed in 1970, resulted in the formation of the National Commission on Materials
Policy which issued its final report in June 1973. The new concern was reflected in
the three "summary directives" of the commission, which were to:

1.   Strike a balance between the "need to produce goods" and the "need to protect the environment" by modifying the materials system so that all resources, including environmental, are paid for by users.

2.   Strive for an equilibrium between the supply of materials and the demand for their use by increasing primary materials production and by conserving materials through accelerated waste recycling and greater efficiency-of-use of materials.

3.   Manage materials policy more effectively by recognizing the complex inter-relationships of the materials-energy-environment system so that laws, executive orders, and administrative practices reinforce policy and not counteract it.[19]

In 1972, a study was completed by the Battelle Memorial Institute, Columbus (Ohio) Laboratories, for the National Association of Secondary Material Industries (N.A.S.M.I.) and the United States Environmental Protection Agency (EPA).[20] Using data on the flow of selected materials in 1969, the study identified numerous opportunities for recycling resources that otherwise were being disposed of as waste.

Perhaps the most dramatic influence pushing the public and its institutions toward an awareness of the need to recycle and conserve was the perception that the nation, notwithstanding its ever increasing gross national product (GNP) — in 1970, slightly less that 1 trillion dollars — was moving from an era of abundant stores of food, energy, metals, timber, and other materials, to one of relative scarcity. How could such a vision occur in the midst of obvious abundance?

The answer jumped out at anyone who familiarized himself with the character of exponential growth. (Refer to Table 1.2 in Chapter 1.) World population growth rates in the 1960s and early 1970s promised to add another worldful of people to the present one in just 35 years. In the United States, where in the late-1960s the population grew slower than in the rest of the world, another 200 million Americans were expected to be added in 70 years to a base of 200 million which had accumulated over four centuries.[21]

If population growth rates were unprecedented, energy and material consumption rates were even more awesome. The United States in 1970 held about 6 percent of the world's population, but consumed 34 percent of all energy used in the world that year. In 1968, the United States produced 23.9 percent of the world's total of 31 selected minerals and consumed 27.9 percent of the world supply.[22]

In short, a society that had been enjoying a 4.5 percent growth rate in the demand for energy and a 3.5 percent growth rate in the GNP was inevitably headed toward shortages despite a relatively low national population growth rate of 1.4 percent per year (1961-1968).

It should be noted that the word "shortage" has meaning only in relation to time, place, prevailing economics, and point of view. Even while discussing energy and food "shortages" in 1972 and 1973, Americans used more resources than any other people in the world.

Opportunities for Materials Recycling

During materials shortages, recycling essential materials is an effective way to extend their use. Even when evidence is lacking that shortages exist, recycling may

TABLE 7.5. Energy Savings from Recycling

Material	Energy Required (coal equivalent kwh/ton)[1]		Saved by Recycling (kwh/ton)	Available for Recycling in 1967 (million tons, approximate)	Possible Energy Savings from Recycling (billion kwh)
	Using Primary Sources	Using Secondary Sources			
Aluminum[2]	64,000	1,300–2,000	62,000	1.0	62
Steel[3]	14,000	6,500	7,500	27	202
Paper[4]	5,000	1,500	3,500	35	122
Total energy savings from recycling					.386

[1]These calculations assume an electric power generating efficiency of about 30 percent.
[2]The two material sources are 50 percent bauxite and aluminum scrap.
[3]For one ton of finished steel. For raw steel, divide figures by 1.5.
[4]The secondary figures is not for a process that uses 100 percent waste paper. Rather, it reflects the saving gained for each ton of waste paper that is substituted for virgin pulp in the regular process.

Source: National Commission on Materials Policy, June 1973.

still be an important way to reduce the energy flow and environmental damage that accompany the production of goods from virgin materials. In times of energy shortages, energy conservation can be the main justification for recycling, as enormous opportunities for saving energy exist in recycling. (Table 7.5)

Virgin Copper Processing

Copper smelting and refining offer a good example. Processing of copper from ore not only consumes great amounts of energy, but it is often a source of serious air and water pollution.

The average copper ore mined in the United States in 1970 contained about 0.6 percent copper.[23] In some cases ores with as little as 0.3 percent copper are being mined,[24] but generally commercial ore grades now range from 0.5 percent to 1.2 percent.[25] Formerly far richer ores were mined, but most large reserves have long since been exhausted. As mining companies move to the lower grade ores, energy requirements go up dramatically. For example, according to Oak Ridge National Laboratory, processing a ton of copper from 1.0 percent ore requires 15,193 kilowatt hours of energy, while a ton of 0.3 percent ore requires 29,766 kilowatt hours, almost twice as much energy.[26]

Figure 7.8 shows the mass and energy flows in the production of a single ton of elemental copper during the late 1960s. Because of the ore's low grade, tremendous amounts of rock had to be moved, more than for any other mineral mined. In order to mine 152.6 tons of 0.65 percent copper ore, an average of 302 tons of overburden (the soil or rock overlying a deposit) which is the first residual or by-product, had to be moved aside and stored in large piles. While this residual remains relatively inert in dry regions, it can become a pollutant in areas of higher rainfall where salts leach from broken rock and disturbed soils and flow into nearby waterways. Piles of overburden can also be costly to the extent that they cover valuable agricultural lands. In 1970, along with 2,269,000 tons of pure copper, the copper mining industry produced 607 million tons of overburden and 258 million tons of tailings (the refuse material separated as residue in the preparation of an ore). If spread uniformly to a depth of one foot, the 1970 ore and waste rocks together would cover an area of 838 square miles. The 865-million-ton total represents one year's production. Each year the amount grows.

After its removal from the ground, the 152.6 tons of ore are crushed, then ground to a fine powder by processes that consume about 8,800 kilowatt hours of energy per ton of copper. Next, the powdered ore is put into a flotation tank and mixed with a chemical agent in a slurry. Copper and iron sulfide particles cling to the agent, float to the top of the slurry, and are skimmed off. The energy cost of flotation is 820 kilowatt hours per ton of copper. A residual from this process, 151 tons of dustlike tailings high in sulfides, can become a pollutant if blown about or drained into waterways.

The copper concentrate, now weighing 1.6 tons, enters a three-stage smelting process using 7,244 kilowatt hours. The major polluting residual, 2.4 tons of sulfur dioxide, is produced at this stage. Some sulfur dioxide is recovered by conversion to elemental sulfur or sulfuric acid and used in copper refining. Most is dissipated into the atmosphere.

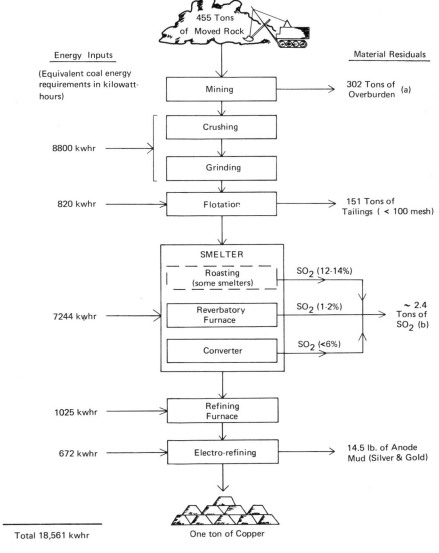

7.8. Mass and Energy Flow in the Processing of One Ton of Copper from 0.65% Sulfide Ore. *Source*: Oak Ridge National Laboratory Report NSF-EP-24, Oak Ridge, Tennessee, 1972.

a   Private communication from H. H. Kellogg, Henry Krumb School of Mines. Columbia University, New York (January 1973).

b   Deduced from (a) data in "Control Techniques for Sulfur Dioxide Air Pollutant," Public Health Service Report, Department of Health, Education, and Welfare, 1969, (b) draft of "New Source Performance Standards Technical Report: Copper, Lead and Zinc Smelters" Environmental Protection Agency, October 1972, (c) Oak Ridge National Laboratory Report, NSF-EP-24, Oak Ridge, Tennessee, 1972

After smelting, the copper, now 98 percent pure, goes to a refining furnace where 1,025 kilowatt hours of energy are used, and then to an electro-refining process, using 672 kilowatt hours. The product is one ton of pure copper, plus anode "mud." The mud is not a residual, but a resource insofar as it yields enough gold, silver, and other rare elements to pay the costs of refining. The total energy requirement, expressed as equivalent coal energy,[27] to process about one ton of pure copper is 18,561 kilowatt hours.

Missing from Figure 7.8 is the flow of water through copper processing. Also missing are energy used in transporting materials from one process to the next and residuals produced in the production of energy.

The Copper Scrap Cycle. In 1969, the United States consumed 3,271,000 short tons of copper, of which domestic ores accounted for 44.9 percent, or 1,469,000 tons, and "old" and "new" scrap constituted 42.0 percent, or 1,375,000 tons. Imports and other sources accounted for the balance, 13.1 percent, or 427,000 tons.[28]

It is important to note that copper and most other metal scrap is graded qualitatively along the general lines shown in Figure 7.9. "New" (or "home") scrap is generated in the production and fabrication of elemental copper. Its form is usually pure copper, highly concentrated and easily recycled. "Industrial" scrap, turnings and trimmings of relatively pure material produced during commodity manufacture, also is easily recycled. "Old" (or "obsolete") scrap is pure copper or copper alloy which has been built into a useful product — usually with several other elements, as in a radio or an automobile — and which is discarded after its useful life. Old scrap comes in several grades. Radiator copper, for example, is a recognized grade easily removed from old cars and recycled. Other grades, such as the electrical wire components of cars or radios, are not so easily recovered and often are lost.[29]

How much copper theoretically available for recycling was not recycled in 1969? The Battelle study showed that old and new copper scrap recycled in 1969 was 61 percent of the amount theoretically available for recycling. That meant that 966,400 tons were not recycled.[30] The Battelle estimate was arrived at by calculating the copper actually in use in commodities that year and estimating the normal life span of the commodities.

If 966,400 tons of scrap copper were not recycled, where were they? They had been disposed of in dumps and landfill sites and dissipated into the environment as chemicals, small particles, or alloys. An informal experiment was undertaken by the Leonardo Seminar to test empirically whether copper in any abundance was actually present in the urban environment. One member of the Seminar picked up copper in his spare time, usually while walking or bicycling between home and office. He observed three rules: he took only that which was obviously lost or discarded (that is, he did not steal); he did not trespass; and he refused to get his shoes unnecessarily muddy. In a few months in 1973, he accumulated thirty pounds of copper metal, mainly in the form of insulated wire, but also in the form of old plumbing parts, screws, pen and pencil parts, cosmetic cases, spent cartridges, flashing and molding, and brass buttons.

From the standpoint of copper users, it may not have been important in 1969 to

ORDER IN WHICH VARIOUS TYPES OF SCRAP ARE RECYCLED

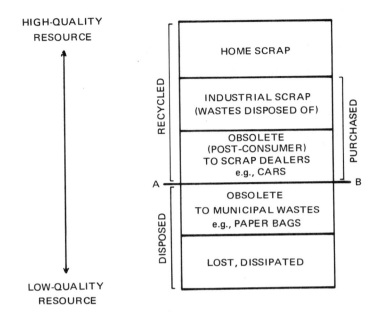

7.9   Types of Scrap Material. Normally the high quality scrap generated by refining or fabricating processes is recycled first. Then high grade obsolete scrap such as battery lead or structural steel is recycled. Some material — such as the mercury in stack effluents, the steel in sunken ships or the small copper parts in worn out home appliances — is lost forever. *Source: Material Needs and the Environment Today and Tomorrow*, Final Report of the National Communion of Materials Policy, 1973.

lose almost a million tons of copper. For one thing, the price of copper was relatively low that year, reflecting ample supply. For another, there were fewer essential uses for copper. Plastics and aluminum were still making inroads on copper as substitutes for copper plumbing and electrical wiring. What was important, however, was that when the nation threw away copper, it threw away energy. This was a significant loss to a people that were soon to see their options as an increasing reliance either on dirty or scarce fossil fuels, or on nuclear power with its problems of radioactivity, waste heat, and radioactive waste disposal.

What was the energy loss in throwing away almost a million tons of copper a year? It takes about 18,561 kilowatt hours of energy to process 152.6 tons of 0.65 percent copper ore into a ton of pure copper; only 9.3 percent of that energy (1,727 kilowatt hours) is needed to remelt scrap copper.[31] Thus, for each ton of copper recycled, about 91 percent of the energy used in primary production from a 0.65 percent ore could be saved, or about 17,000 kilowatt hours a ton. If the 966,400 tons of copper theoretically available for recycling in 1969 had been regathered and reprocessed, savings in energy would have approached 16.4 billion kilowatt hours of equivalent coal energy. This is enough energy to supply the residential electricity demands of a city of 750,000 population, a Milwaukee, for example, for one year at 1969 electrical use levels of about 6,500 kilowatt hours per capita.[32]

Recycling Other Materials

So much for copper. What about steel, paper, aluminum, all other elements wasted in landfill sites, or which had become pollutants? A similar calculation was made for aluminum in the Battelle study. In 1969, 1,159,000 tons of aluminum theoretically available for recycling were not recycled. The Battelle study said:

> Of the estimated 1.3 million tons of aluminum becoming obsolete, only 175,000 tons of aluminum were reclaimed in 1969, or in other words, only 13 percent of the aluminum becoming obsolete was recycled. However, it is likely that the amount of old aluminum scrap readily available to the recycling industry is actually much smaller because:
> 1. Some items, especially aircraft, are exported then not scrapped in the United States
> 2. Some items such as aluminum cans and other packaging items are widely disseminated and usually are not collected
> 3. Some obsolete items such as certain military aircraft are being stored (for use during emergencies) rather than being scrapped
> 4. The data are not corrected for recovery yields.[33]

Though aluminum was recycled at a rate far below the 61 percent for copper, potential energy savings from recycling scrap aluminum was four times greater than for copper. According to the Oak Ridge National Laboratory study,[34] 63,895 kilowatt hours of energy are needed to process one ton of aluminum from bauxite that contains 50 percent alumina. On the other hand, from 1,300 to 2,000 kilowatt hours are needed to reprocess a ton of scrap aluminum.[35] This represents savings of at least 61,895 kilowatt hours of energy for each ton recycled. If all 1,159,000 tons of aluminum thrown away in 1969 had been recycled, the nation would have saved 71.8 billion kilowatt hours, enough energy to supply the residential electricity demands of a city of more than 3 million population for a year.

The above examples point out how much energy could theoretically be saved. There are other savings of significant importance. By recycling copper now discarded, much pollution could be avoided. For each ton of recycled copper, the generation of 302 tons of overburden, 151 tons of tailing, and 2.4 tons of sulfur dioxide could be avoided. The National Commission of Materials Policy addressed the subject of savings in energy, raw materials, and pollutants in its final report:

> . . . the use of primary materials consumes more energy per ton of production than secondary materials, as demonstrated by studies of steel, copper, aluminum, and paper production [Table 7.5]. About 2 percent of the total U.S. energy demand could be saved by the recycling of available steel, aluminum, and paper. An alternative method of resource recovery, burning municipal wastes, would satisfy about 3 percent of the Nation's energy needs.

Finally, the use of primary materials loads the environment with atmospheric emissions and solid and waterborne wastes, and increases the demand for process water, as determined by studies of steel, glass, and paper manufacture.

If it were possible to sell all the paper available in municipal waste each year at today's secondary paper prices, the total mass would command a selling price of half a billion dollars. Recycling this material also would save the nation an estimated million tons of air pollution, as papermakers using virgin material inherently produce more pollution than those using secondary materials.[36]

Table 7.6 shows the deferred dollar value and environmental damage resulting from failure to recycle. The above examples show that opportunities exist to conserve enormous amounts of energy through recycling. The examples are insufficient insofar as they do not account for other energy costs of recycling or virgin processing. For example, the energy costs of "mining" the metal from either the virgin ore deposit or the urban scene, including dumps and landfill sites, are not included.

Furthermore, not all of the copper or aluminum theoretically available for recycling can ever be recycled. A portion of it seems lost forever: the hunter's spent cartridge that is plowed under a cornfield, the copper sulfate used for algae control on inland lakes that now lies in the lake bottom sediments, and the low grade alloys that require re-refining.

A Practical Example

The above examples, while illustrating opportunities for saving materials, energy, and environmental costs, are not directly helpful in showing how to institute recycling practices within the complex systems of materials processing and economics. Fortunately, there seems to be progress along these lines as well. A University of Illinois researcher, Bruce Hannon, in making a complete energy analysis of beer and soft drink packaging, has shown how precise energy-cost calculations can be used to improve energy efficiencies.

His report, "System Energy and Recycling: A Study of the Beverage Industry,"[37] applies the laws of conservation of mass and energy to the packaging industry. "If any generality can be gained from [this] example, it is that recycling of mass should be accomplished at the earliest opportunity, in order to use the least mass and the least energy of the alternatives available to perform a desired service," Hannon wrote.[38]

Hannon concluded that enterprises should plan for least-energy-consuming systems. But before one can do so, one must analyze precisely how much energy is used in any process, Hannon said. He analyzed the energy required in various packages in which beer, soft drinks, and milk are sold, including aluminum cans, steel cans with aluminum ends, steel cans, returnable glass bottles, throwaway glass bottles, paper and plastic cartons.

Hannon calculated the energy required in each phase of each packaging system, including energy used to acquire raw materials, transport them, convert them to packages, fill and market them, and then dispose of them, either as residuals in

TABLE 7.6. Costs of Not Recycling 225 Million Tons of Municipal Waste

Material	Amount Available in Municipal Waste[1] (million tons)	Amount Recoverable (%)	Apparent Value (million dollars)	Municipal Solid Waste (million tons)	Some Environmental Impacts That Could Be Avoided	
					Air Pollution (thousand tons)	Water Pollution (thousand tons)
Paper	34	45	506	34	930[3]	62[2,3]
Glass	13	70	126	13	50	NA
Ferrous metals	15	90	183	15	1,560	750
Nonferrous metals	1	67	180	1	NA	NA
Totals	63		995	63	2,540	812

[1]These figures assume a total of 225 million tons of municipal waste.
[2]The water pollution figure is for suspended solids; BOD is not calculated.
[3]Low grade paper from repulped waste paper rather than from unbleached kraft pulp. Assumes 1.1 tons of waste paper is needed to make 1 ton of pulp.

Source: National Commission on Materials Policy, June 1973.

landfills or litter, or as recycled materials reintroduced into the system. Among his findings:

> The energy required to deliver a soft drink to a consumer in a throwaway glass container was 3.3 times as much as for returnable bottles, assuming returnables were reused 15 times.
>
> Combined steel and aluminum soft drink cans required 2.4 times more energy than 12-ounce returnable bottles.
>
> Beer in 12-ounce throwaway bottles and steel cans with aluminum tops and bottoms used 3.1 and 3.0 times more energy, respectively, than a 12-ounce returnable bottle reused 19 times.
>
> Half-gallon paper milk containers used 1.6 times the energy of their returnable glass counterparts.[39]

Americans paid a premium for the convenience of throwing away beverage containers. At the time of Hannon's study, soft drinks in disposable cans or bottles cost 30 percent more than the same drinks sold in returnable containers in Illinois. Beer in throwaway containers cost more than beer in returnable bottles, although the price difference was not enough to discourage the use of throwaways, that is, to offset their convenience. A greater differential might have done so, Hannon suggested. And a greater differential would have occurred had the full costs of production been paid directly by consumers.[40]

Hannon wrote:

> Added to this [the purchase price] are litter pickup, hauling and landfill costs paid by the consumer through monthly billings from trash haulers and state and municipal taxes. There are, in addition, the environmental costs of material and energy production paid in terms of health and aesthetic losses such as lung damage from power plant emissions and land strip mined for coal. Were these costs tabulated and presented to the consumers at the time of purchase, consumers would at least know the true cost of packaging convenience and might choose to buy less expensive returnable containers.[41]

What was more dramatic in his analysis, however, were Hannon's conclusions regarding opportunities for saving energy.

> If the beverage industry were converted entirely to returnable containers, the 1970 container system energy, which accounts for 0.48 percent of the total U.S. energy demand, would be reduced by about 40 percent.[42]

If the United States is in fact moving from a period of energy abundance (low cost energy) to scarcity (high cost energy) and if it is moving from a time when external costs of production of energy are to be passed to consumers, then energy cost might very well affect consumer prices in major ways and producers might hunt for ways to reduce their energy costs. As of 1973, energy costs were going up but had not yet affected beverage packaging. The trend set by the brewers was to move to all-aluminum cans, which were the most energy intensive of all beverage container choices.

The Waste Problem

In 1973, energy conservation had emerged as the most compelling reason for altering economic and materials processes to permit recycling of greater amounts of materials. This emergence followed by several years a public move, associated with "environmental awareness," which brought pressures on government and industry to find ways to reduce material waste.

That waste was substantial. According to the National Commission on Materials Policy:

> The total volume by weight of solid wastes in the United States in 1971 reached 4.4 billion tons. Most solid wastes originate with agriculture and livestock. Other volumes come from mining and industrial processes. A little less than 6 percent, or 230 million tons, is urban waste. Only three-fourths of this is collected.
>
> Although wastes from homes, businesses, and institutions are a small part of the total, they are the most offensive and dangerous to health when they accumulate near residential centers.
>
> The [urban] solid waste collected annually includes 30 million tons of paper and paper products; 4 million tons of plastics; 100 million tires; 30 billion bottles; 60 billion cans; millions of tons of demolition debris, grass, and tree trimmings; food wastes; and millions of discarded major appliances.[43]

Further, the commission said:

> Solid waste tonnages are growing three times as fast as population, about 5 percent per year. Nonreturnable container production is steadily increasing as is disposable plastic packaging. A study for the plastics industry in 1967 estimated that tonnages would increase by about 85 percent in five years. It is estimated that per capita consumption of packaging materials will reach 660 pounds by 1976, up from 580 pounds in 1970.[44]

Obviously, such an inefficient system of materials and energy use continues only because the nation has not bumped into critical shortages of essentials and because society avoids even minor inconveniences. But, as Bruce Hannon said in his study, "We must also soon question the need of the quantity consumed in providing a given quality of life. In other words, there is an extremely important distinction between evaluating system efficiency and evaluating system energy flow; the former is primarily an engineering matter. The latter is mainly a societal one."[45]

Why the Waste?

If so much could be gained in energy savings through conservation and recycling of materials, why wasn't it? The answer was that the United States had committed itself deeply to policies that encouraged a heavy flow of both energy and materials through its systems, but did not encourage reuse or conservation. By mid-1973, several observers identified economic practices and public policies working against recycling.

The League of Women Voters of the United States published a pamphlet in 1972 entitled "Recycle?"[46] in which four categories of obstacles to recycling were outlined. They were:

1. Pricing which favored the use of virgin materials by excluding environmental costs of production. Furthermore, some prices were kept artifically low by public policies which granted, in effect, a competitive edge to businesses that mined, grazed, pumped oil, or took timber from the public lands.

2. Federal tax provisions which favored the use of virgin materials through: (a) capital gains treatment for some profits; (b) depreciation allowances which permitted fast write-off for much capital cost of mine development; and (c) depletion allowances applicable to a broad range of minerals.

3. Shipping policies which set higher (some said discriminatory) freight rates for secondary or recycled materials than for virgin materials. Prompt deliveries of scrap also were hampered by a shortage of gondola cars. The fleet had decreased by more than 35 percent from 1955 to 1970.

4. Miscellaneous laws and regulations, such as purchasing requirements, which called for use of virgin materials in products rather than concentrating on performance standards, regardless of material source. State and local licensing and zoning laws often imposed barriers to the secondary materials industry by prohibiting its operations in certain areas.

The League's booklet contained a "shopping list" of possible encouragements for recycling and conservation, falling broadly into two groups: those designed to stimulate demand for recycled materials and those designed to overcome obstacles to recycling.

For example, taxes might be imposed on virgin materials, reducing their price advantage. Such taxes could become general revenue or they could be earmarked to subsidize specific programs of secondary materials processing or upgrading of municipal solid waste systems. Such taxes could be considered deterrent taxes, imposed to limit the use of a material by artificially raising its price, or disposal taxes, levied to cover the cost of product disposal.

Tax benefits now enjoyed by virgin materials industries could be cut or eliminated. These could include capital gains treatment for timber or depletion allowances for minerals. (The concept of depletion allowance was enacted as public policy decades ago on the purported grounds of meeting the needs of an expanding economy and national defense.)

Finally, subsidies could be extended to the secondary materials industry. These might be tax credits to manufacturers who increased use of recycled materials; fast tax write-offs for expensive scrap processing machinery, such as automobile shredders; low cost loans or guaranteed capital to secondary materials industries; or price supports for secondary materials through federal purchase and stockpiling.

Other encouragements for recycling might come from the Interstate Commerce Commission in the form of actions to narrow the gap between low freight rates granted virgin materials industries and high rates paid by scrap industries. Furthermore, government could encourage scrap exports or it could specify, in its own purchasing, that it would accept only recycled materials in some products such as paper.

The League study, a general one, surveyed the state of the art of recycling, identified social and economic barriers, and suggested policy which might facilitate recycling. The Final Report of the National Commission on Materials Policy,[47] published in June 1973, in its review of obstacles to recycling, argued that stimulating demand for recyclables was the most effective strategy. It suggested three approaches: new mechanisms for concentrating valuable materials from municipal wastes at lower costs; new incentives for disposers of goods to prepare, deliver, and perhaps pay for recycling; and encouragement of product designs for ease of recycling.

While the commission rejected suggestions that tax or pricing benefits now extended to virgin materials industries be withdrawn (it did the opposite; it recommended more benefits), it nonetheless concluded that secondary materials ought to be on equal footing with their virgin counterparts. Its conclusion was that

> increased recycling would result if primary and secondary materials were on an equal footing in the market place. All national resources should receive equal treatment. Equalization should create conditions for increased competition between primary and secondary materials. Market forces would determine their relative levels of use.[48]

In general, the commission would accomplish such equalization by extending tax benefits to the secondary materials industries for the purchase of high cost processing machinery; by offering tax incentives to industries, such as steel mills, for using higher proportions of scrap; and by eliminating the freight rate differential between scrap and virgin materials. Furthermore, the commission called for increased federally sponsored research on new recovery technologies.

A more specific identification of obstacles to recycling was made by the Battelle Memorial Institute in its study on solid waste utilization.[49] The study concentrated on recycling aluminum, copper, lead, zinc, nickel, stainless steel, precious metals, paper, and textiles. It identified five general obstacles common to minerals recycling. They were: (1) irrational customer specification and discriminatory government procurement policies; (2) the mixed and highly diluted character of post-consumer solid wastes; (3) lack of know-how in purchasing, installing, using, and maintaining recycling equipment, resulting in process inefficiencies; (4) inadequte or unavailable equipment for waste recovery, forcing a reliance upon uneconomical methods of waste recovery; and (5) depletion allowances which created an unfair price advantage for primary materials.[50]

The Battelle study also described in detail the recycling, or secondary materials, industry in the United States.[51] Unlike some primary producing industries, which were few in number and vertically concentrated, the secondary materials industries numbered hundreds of small firms, scattered wherever large amounts of scrap were generated, mainly in the large cities of the Atlantic and Great Lakes states.

The Battelle study also provided great detail for each material analyzed. In its study on copper,[52] supply and demand for both primary and secondary copper were analyzed. The recycling part of the study included processing of scrap, marketing, and recycling rates for each type of copper scrap. It identified barriers in recycling each major category of scrap and recommended specific "high" and "low priority" measures that might increase recycling. It broke down types of copper scrap into five categories: "Copper wire and tube," "magnet wire," "cartridge brass," "other brass," and "copper used as an additive in other metals." It estimated for each the short tons and percentages not recycled in 1969, and analyzed why it was not. For example, in the wire and tube category, only 18 percent, or 151,800 short tons, was not recycled.[53] The study revealed that copper plumbing has a useful life of 60 to 65 years, and wire used by utilities is in place 50 years or thereabouts. Almost all of both types is recycled. However, wire and tubing widely scattered in consumer products such as refrigerators or air-conditioners are less efficiently recycled and frequently lost. Of the total category, perhaps 5 to 10 percent inevitably must be lost. In fact, 18 percent was lost. "This appears to be a promising area in which to increase recycling," the study said.[54]

The conclusion was different for copper used as an additive in minor amounts to strengthen other metals, such as steel. It was almost impossible to separate the copper, usually present in amounts of less than 1 percent, from such alloys. Therefore almost all of the 96,900 short tons of copper so used in 1969 was lost, and there was little potential for improving recovery.[55]

While the Battelle study concentrated on specific materials, the U.S. Environmental Protection Agency analyzed recycling problems of a specific product in its 1972 publication "The Automobile Cycle: An Environmental and Resource Reclamation Problem."[56] The EPA analyzed problems in recycling, starting with the point of manufacture, where many materials are brought together to form a product with little thought to recycling those materials later. The EPA analyzed why many cars were abandoned on streets rather than redirected into the materials flow, a social and economic problem. The auto scrap industry also was analyzed and the route of auto scrap was traced to its ultimate users, the steel industry and foundries. The EPA study recommended scores of strategies to improve the system — that is, to recycle all cars.

For example, government could increase recycling by levying a disposal tax on cars or by charging car buyers a deposit to be returned when the owner showed proof that he had properly disposed of his car. Bounties could be paid to people who collected and routed abandoned autos to salvage yards. Subsidies could be paid to dismantlers, scrap processors, steel mills, or scrap exporters. Government could use its regulatory power to impose fines for abandoned automobiles. It could impose uniformity on methods for transferring titles of old cars, a complex problem that results in increased abandonment. Government could ban the use of certain materials in cars, or encourage auto design that allowed easy and complete removal of nonferrous metals.

In summary, barriers to efficient resource use were institutional, economic, and physical. If the United States threw away usable resources and wasted energy, it did so because thousands of individual decisions at all levels were made by a variety of people who considered problems piecemeal as they arose. Such decisions were made in the context of limited institutional, economic, and physical systems that had evolved over time and changed slowly. In general, lavish or wasteful uses of resources resulted from a society in which energy and materials were abundant, and therefore of low cost. A society that perceived itself moving from abundance to shortages would, it was presumed, adopt institutional, economic, and physical systems to discourage waste. But, if the movement from abundance to shortage was abrupt, the institutional and economic change could be disruptive. The next two chapters, "The Bigger They Come . . ." and "Small Steps to Solve Big Problems," suggest ways in which disruptions might be avoided.

References

1. Allen V. Kneese, Robert U. Ayres, and Ralph C. d'Arge, *Economics and the Environment* (Baltimore: Johns Hopkins Press, 1970), pp. 4-7.
2. *Pollutants* can, however, include the desired product as well as the leftover residuals. DDT is an example.
3. A BTU, or British Thermal Unit, is the amount of energy required to raise the temperature of one pound of water one degree Fahrenheit.
4. "1972 U.S. Energy Use Continued Upward," news release, Bureau of Mines, Department of Interior, March 10, 1973.
5. Office of Emergency Preparedness, *The Potential for Energy Conservation*, Staff Report OEP 4102-0009 (Washington, D.C.: U.S. Government Printing Office, 1972).
6. See notes 8, 9, 10 and 11 below, and accompanying text.
7. C. A. Berg, "Energy Conservation Through Effective Utilization," *Science* 181:130 (July 13, 1973).
8. *Minimum Property Standards for One and Two Living Units*, FHA Report 300, Interior Revision 51A, (Washington, D.C.: U.S. Government Printing Office, 1971).
9. Eric Hirst and John C. Moyers, "Efficiency of Energy Use in the United States," *Science* 179:1300-1302 (March 30, 1973).
10. John C. Moyers, *The Value of Thermal Insulation in Residential Construction: Economics and the Conservation of Energy*, Oak Ridge National Laboratory Report NSF-EP-9 (Oak Ridge, Tenn.: 1971), pp. 15-24.
11. Hirst and Moyers, "Efficiency of Energy Use," p. 1301.
12. W. K. Foell and J. E. Rushton, "Energy Use in Wisconsin," Working Paper No. 4, Institute for Environmental Studies, University of Wisconsin (Madison: 1972), p. 39.
13. Eric Hirst, *Energy Consumption for Transportation in the U.S.*, Oak Ridge National Laboratory Report NSF-EP-15 (Oak Ridge, Tenn.: 1972), p. 11.
14. Ibid., p. 13.
15. Foell and Rushton, "Energy Use in Wisconsin," pp. 13-18.
16. Hirst, *Energy Consumption for Transportation*, pp. 11-13; 19-20.

17. M. A. Caruso, "Energy Use for Transportation in Wisconsin: A Mathematical Model," unpublished M. S. thesis, University of Wisconsin, Nuclear Engineering Department, Madison, August 1973.
18. Resource Recovery Act of 1970, 42 U.S.C. § §3251-3254f, 3256-3259 (1970).
19. *Material Needs and the Environment, Today and Tomorrow,* National Commission on Materials Policy Final Report (Washington, D.C.: 1973), p. 14.
20. Battelle Memorial Institute, *A Study to Identify Opportunities for Increased Solid Waste Utilization,* 9 vols. (Columbus, Ohio: 1972).
21. "1970 World Population Data Sheet," Population Reference Bureau, Inc., Washington, D.C., April 1970. More recent census data suggest that the U.S. population is approaching a doubling time of 126 years. (Personal communication from Henry Krebs, Research Analyst, Statistical Services, Wisconsin Division of Health, Madison, Wisconsin, October 1974.)
22. *Towards a National Materials Policy,* National Commission on Materials Policy Interim Report (Washington, D.C.: 1972), p. 4.
23. D. P. Cox, R. G. Schmidt, J. D. Vine, H. Kirkemo, E. B. Tourtelot, and M. Fleischer, "Copper", in D. A. Brobst and W. A. Pratt, eds., *United States Mineral Resources,* U.S.G.S. Paper 820 (Washington, D.C.: U.S. Government Printing Office, 1973), p. 166.
24. Ibid., p. 170.
25. Personal communication from Eugene Cameron, Geology Department, University of Wisconsin, Madison, Wisconsin.
26. J. C. Bravard, H. B. Flora II, and Charles Portal, *Energy Expenditures Associated with the Production and Recycle of Metals;* Oak Ridge National Laboratory Report NSF-EP-24 (Oak Ridge, Tenn.: 1972), Table 12, p. 34.
27. Energy used to process copper comes from a variety of sources. Total energy used has been converted here to the amount of energy used if only coal were burned, that is, "equivalent coal energy."
28. Battelle, *Opportunities for Increased Solid Waste Utilization,* vol. III, Figure 1, p. 12.
29. *Material Needs and the Environment,* p. 4D-7.
30. Battelle, *Opportunities for Increased Solid Waste Utilization,* vol. I, Table III, p. 21.
31. The 16.4 billion kilowatt hours refer to the initial energy needed to produce electricity. Since the average efficiency of converting a primary fuel (oil, coal) to electrical energy is approximately 33 percent, the end use electrical energy is only one-third of the amount of the primary energy.
32. Bravard, Flora II, and Portal, *Energy Expenditures,* Table 14, p. 39.
33. Battelle, *Opportunities for Increased Solid Waste Utilization,* vol. II, pp. 44, 46.
34. Bravard, Flora II, and Portal, *Energy Expenditures,* Table 4, p. 15.
35. Ibid., p. 19.
36. *Material Needs and the Environment,* pp. 4D-8, 4D-9.
37. Bruce Hannon, "System Energy and Recycling: A Study of the Beverage Industry," Center for Advanced Computation, Doc. no. 23, University of Illinois, Champaign-Urbana, 1972, revised March 17, 1973.
38. Ibid., p. 1.
39. Ibid., Table 9.
40. See Chapter 5, "Faustian and Other Bargains," for a discussion of external costs.
41. Hannon, "System Energy and Recycling," pp. 3-4.
42. Ibid., p. 23.
43. *Material Needs and the Environment,* p. 4D-3.
44. Ibid., p. 4D-4.

45. Hannon, "System Energy and Recycling," p. 2.
46. League of Women Voters, "Recycle," League Publication No. 132, (Washington, D.C.: 1972), pp. 11-18.
47. *Material Needs and the Environment.*
48. Ibid.. p 4D-16.
49. Battelle, *Opportunities for Increased Solid Waste Utilization.*
50. Ibid., vol. I, pp. 53-65.
51. Ibid., vol. I, pp. 18-45.
52. Ibid., vol. III.
53. Ibid., vol. III, Table 14, p. 41.
54. Ibid., vol. III, Table 18, p. 48.
55. Ibid.
56. *The Automobile Cycle: An Environmental and Resource Reclamation Problem*, U.S. Environmental Protection Agency (Washington, D.C.: 1972).

8.   The Bigger They Come . . .

"Bigger and better" is a familiar phrase based on the assumption that a thing which is bigger is necessarily better. But as the limits of energy, material resources, and land itself become more apparent, "thinking bigger" is meeting increasing resistance from various quarters. Consumers demand smaller, more efficient cars, and homeowners resist the expansion of highways that will bring accelerated growth and congestion to their cities. This critical questioning of bigness must be extended to all of man's activities, from his huge constructions based on so-called "economies of scale" to his big, one-step remedies for complex problems. It is not so much a matter of always "thinking small"; rather, it is a matter of not always "thinking big."

This chapter will look at the merits of "thinking small" and diversifying our sources of material and energy as a means of (a) conserving matter and energy and (b) increasing stability in our economic system.

Consumer and Producer Attitudes

"Thinking small" should not refer merely to the outside dimensions of a product, but also to the energy and material resources that are consumed in its manufacture, use, and eventual disposal. This implies that if one is conscious of conserving material and energy when manufacturing an item, that is, if he is "thinking small," he will make a product with longevity. He will avoid the material and energy waste of building a product which prematurely deteriorates or becomes obsolete and then must be replaced.

In a world in which material and energy resources are finite, there are no long-term gains from waste. The manufacturer's goal from the standpoint of resource policy should be always to produce an item that will perform the functions for which it is intended as efficiently and esthetically as is reasonably possible and, at the same time, will consume the minimum of energy and material resources.

Most commodities currently in use were not produced with this goal in mind. Automobiles manufactured in the United States vary widely in size and horsepower. There are great differences in the amount of metal, plastic, and rubber used in their manufacture, the amount of gasoline required to power them, and the amount of air pollution they create. Electrical appliances such as refrigerators or air conditioners differ in the efficiency with which they use energy in their operation.[1] Automatic washing machines[2] and dishwashers[3] vary in the efficiency with which they use both energy and water.[4]

Consumers, manufacturers, and government all play a part in determining what goods are in popular use. If government were to take greater responsibility for resource conservation, it might choose to play a more active role in determining what kinds of goods are produced. This action could take several forms: restriction, by statute or regulation, of products or features which are wasteful of resources; adoption of economic policies which would increase the cost to the producer and consumer of inefficient or polluting products; and requirement that manufacturers inform customers of the energy demands of their product.

Restriction of Certain Features and Products

Government is already regulating product form and quality to some extent, without significantly reducing consumer demand for the product.

For example, in order to reduce air pollution, the federal government is now setting emission standards which must be met by new cars before they can be marketed. Standards could be similarly set and enforced for minimum gas mileage, maximum horsepower, maximum weight and maximum outside dimensions if such measures were thought necessary for the preservation of the nation's resources. These standards not only would reduce the energy and material expended in building and powering automobiles but would also reduce energy and materials expended in building and maintaining the nation's highways.

Influencing Economic Factors

In the extraction of resources and manufacture of goods, some costs of production — such as air and water pollution — are not paid by the producer. The National Materials Policy Commission and a committee of the National Academy of Sciences have both recommended that, in order to encourage material and energy conservation, all costs of production, be charged to the producer and included in the price of the product.[5,6] Thus the price of the product would include the producer's costs for maintaining pollution abatement equipment or paying effluent charges.

Even while talking about the need to conserve, today's government continues to indirectly encourage waste by subsidizing many producers and manufacturers through loans and tax benefits. By ending questionable subsidies to some industries or by granting subsidies to industries that recycle or use material that otherwise would be wasted, or by a combination of these approaches, government could take positive steps in the direction of conservation.

Information for Consumers

The consumer should be given the opportunity to make an informed choice among available products. Manufacturers could be required to include with each item information which will enable the consumer to compare products on the basis of their energy and resource content or requirements. At a minimum, manufacturers could be required to include with each vehicle and appliance an understandable statement of its size and weight and the amount of energy required to operate it — average miles per gallon for a vehicle and kilowatt-hours per hundred hours of use for electric appliances.

Consumer awareness of the national need to conserve resources and energy is growing as the hazards of a contrary course become better understood and accepted. We must encourage a public desire to "keep up with the Joneses" by consuming and wasting less rather than by consuming and wasting more. But this desire will be of no avail unless consumers are provided the facts on which to make informed choices.

Economies of Scale

Energy and material conservation are also possible through "economies of scale," that is, designs of structures or systems at the optimum size for maximum efficiency. Optimum size is determined by factors such as the task to be accomplished and the materials and equipment that are available. A 250-ton truck with wheels that are six feet high is a more efficient vehicle than a 10-ton truck for moving coal in some open-pit or strip mines.[7] This does not mean, however, that a 700-ton truck would be even more efficient in the mine, and obviously all such trucks would be inefficient vehicles for the delivery of groceries.

While economy of scale implies that increased efficiency can accompany a move to either larger or smaller scale, it is seldom that an operation moves in the latter direction. In some cases "economy of scale" is simply a euphemism for "bigger is better"; in all cases the claim of economy of scale requires proof. To determine at what scale economy really occurs, more than internal costs must be evaluated. External costs including such factors as vulnerability and maintenance of competing alternatives must be considered also.

Cost

For owners of a proposed 1,000 megawatt coal generating plant to prove an economy of scale, costs for plant management and purchase and maintenance of generation and antipollution equipment must be shown to be less than costs for two 500 megawatt plants.

Moreover, while an economy of scale may grant the utility or corporation manager the greatest economic and engineering efficiency, the same scale may be simultaneously causing waste of resources outside the system. These costs incurred by persons other than the producer or consumer of a product must be considered also. For example, use of heavy coal trucks on local highways may reduce the direct cost per ton of transporting coal to the consumer and may be an economy of scale for the coal company, but in some parts of Appalachia, 40 percent of the maintenance budgets for state and county roads go to repairing damages caused by coal-truck traffic.[8] When total costs to society are summed, are there "economies"?

Vulnerability

As a system gets bigger it tends to impose uniformity on its component parts for its own administrative convenience if not for efficiency. However, the fewer and more concentrated the sources of a necessity, the more dependent we are on each source and the more vulnerable we become.

Modern agriculture presents examples of the pitfalls of uniformity. As agriculture has moved to larger scales and greater mechanization, there has been demand for greater uniformity of crops, including wheat. When the grain is of uniform size and the plants mature simultaneously, planting and harvesting by machine is more efficient. A uniform product also facilitates milling and baking. Consequently, popularity of a few varieties with very similar characteristics has produced a near monoculture of wheat in parts of the United States.[9] However, as the National Research Council of the National Academy of Sciences points out,

> Uniformity of produce means uniformity in the genetics of the crop. This, in turn, means that a genetically uniform crop is highly likely to pick up any mutant strain of organism that chances to have the capacity to attack it.[10]

Vast acreage of the same variety of wheat enables disease or insects to which the wheat variety is susceptible to spread easily and build to epidemic proportions.

> In recent years the life expectancy of wheat varieties in the Pacific Northwest has been about five years. The variety Elgin was grown for six years before common bunt [fungus] became destructive of it. Elmar replaced Elgin, but within five years it was compromised by another bunt race. Omar replaced Elmar in 1957, but it had to be replaced by Gaines in 1961 because of extreme stripe rust susceptibility....[11]

Obviously, greater diversity in wheat plantings would reduce this vulnerability. But at this point, achieving the desirable level of diversity in the United States would necessitate a return to smaller farms — and drastically reduced production — or a massive administrative network to plan and enforce a diversified planting program. At present, neither choice is a realistically acceptable alternative to a highly productive mechanized monoculture which is planted according to the market report.

Instead, the United States and other wheat-growing nations have devised technologies to anticipate and counteract disease and pest epidemics. Besides chemical control, the major defense is maintenance of a wide diversity of genetic lines, and the constant development of new varieties.

The strategy thus far has been successful, but it remains totally dependent on an advanced technology of plant breeding and communication. The Ford Foundation, for example, has organized an "early warning system" for wheat disease.[12] This consists of a number of Regional Disease and Insect Screening Nurseries (RDISN) which are located from India to Morocco to Western Europe at sites where severe disease epidemics occur naturally each year. New races of insects and pathogens with the potential to become future problems are frequently found at an early date in these "hot spots." This screening program also provides an opportunity to detect wheat varieties that are resistant to the new pest strains.

The International Rice Research Institute (IRRI) has a similar network of nurseries in the Philippines and Asia where rice varieties are screened for susceptibility to new strains of blast and other pathogens.[13]

These warning systems enable farmers to remove susceptible varieties from production the following year, thus avoiding crop loss and slowing the epidemic's spread.

For some crops, such as fruit and vegetables, greater diversity is possible and is frequently accomplished (though as often by accident as by intent).

However, in other cases, opportunities to diversify have been available but have been brushed aside for a single and ultimately regrettable choice. The intensive use of insecticides in agricultural pest control is a classic example:

> Pesticides emerged rather slowly and in a crude form out of the nineteenth century. Then with surprising suddenness they evolved into compounds having spectacular toxicity. They proliferated enormously.[14]

> At first there were only minor hints of trouble, but these rapidly grew more alarming. Commercial chemical products, once touted as panaceas, became ineffectual on the newly resistant pest populations. This was followed by an increasingly accelerated effort by the chemical industry to develop substitutes. Cross-resistance appeared.... Pest control expenses increased.[15]

Pest control for many crops began to follow the pattern seen in cotton:

> After a variable number of years in the . . . heavy use of pesticides, a series of events occurs. More frequent applications of pesticides are needed to get effective control. The treatments are started earlier in the cotton growing season and extended later into the harvest period. It is notable that the pest populations now resurge rapidly after treatment to new higher levels. The pest populations gradually become so tolerant of a particular pesticide that it becomes useless. Another pesticide is substituted and the pest populations become tolerant to it too, but this happens more rapidly than with the first chemical. At the same time, pests that never caused damage in the area previously, or only occasionally, become serious and regular ravagers of the cotton fields. This combination of pesticide resistance, pest resurgence, and the unleashing of secondary pests, or the induced rise to pest status of species previously innocuous, occasions a greatly increased application of pesticides and causes greatly increased production costs . . . to the point where cotton can no longer be grown profitably. At first only marginal land and marginal farmers are removed from production. Eventually, cotton is no longer profitable to produce in any parts of the area.[16]

This history does not suggest that chemicals should never have been used to reduce insect populations nor does it indicate that the use of chemical pesticides should be completely abandoned in the future. What it does indicate is that attempting to control insect pests by intensive use of a single approach takes insufficient account of ecology and makes crops even more vulnerable, and is therefore unlikely to be successful. It is only through balanced and restrained use of a diversity of methods — an integrated approach — that crop stability can be secured in a complex ecosystem.

For example, integrated control for California cotton pests includes

1. regular field sampling of the number and the stage of development of pest species;

2. determining the threshold at which a pest population causes economic loss;

3. identifying natural enemies (predators and parasites) and their role in controlling pest species;

4. increasing natural enemy populations by creating conditions favorable to their development or raising them in laboratory culture;

5. determining the effectiveness of chemical control measures on pest populations;

6. determining the timing of the insect's development cycle — especially those stages in which it is most damaging to crops and most susceptible to chemical control;

7. identifying cultural and agronomic practices which could be used in pest control (e.g. the depth and time of plowing);

8. developing chemical and microbial controls which are selectively toxic to the pest population.[17]

In the energy area also, vulnerability increases when "all the eggs are in one basket." By building ever larger power plants, electric utility companies try to maintain sufficient standby generating capacity so that they will seldom be required, because of peak electrical demands, to buy electricity from other companies. But as the "optimum size plant" continues to increase in size, vulnerability increases — the chance of severe damage at one large plant becomes more likely than the simultaneous breakdown of three small plants — and even more standby capacity is required.

In addition, each electric utility in the United States is part of an interconnected series of transmission lines, called a "grid," through which power can be transmitted from one utility area to another or from one grid region to another. The vulnerability of this sytem was demonstrated on November 9, 1965, when trouble in one utility area in northern New York State acted through the interconnecting lines to black out 80,000 square miles in the northeastern United States and parts of Canada, an area inhabited by 30 million people.[18] Changes have been made in the system in an effort to prevent a recurrence, and no failures have occurred over such a wide area since that time. In 1973, however, power failed for several hours throughout utility areas in Florida as the result of trouble in one area.

Similarly, fuel oil shortages in several parts of the country in the winter of 1972-1973 and gasoline shortages the following summer caused national concern. It became obvious that heavy reliance on the single fuel, petroleum, could have immediate and severe effects upon one's activities when petroleum products are in short supply.

In all the above examples, the breakdown of a concentrated, uniform system means a loss of energy and materials from the human enterprise. Seeds are planted, fertilizer is applied, the crop is tended and then lost to disease or pests. A region's only super power system breaks down and those who relied on its electricity to refrigerate perishables or operate irrigation pumps may see their season's work destroyed. "Thinking small" and diversifying for the sake of reliability sometimes may be more important than "thinking big" for immediate monetary savings.

Yet, in spite of mounting evidence that our present sources of energy may be inadequate to meet our increasing demands and that our systems for distributing energy are vulnerable to massive breakdown, we seem unwilling to protect ourselves through diversification. We continue to seek increased production of the one form of energy that was dependable in the past, fossil fuel, and the one form that is touted as being capable of meeting our future needs, nuclear.

Total energy use in the United States at the end of 1971 was as follows: petroleum, 44.2 percent; natural gas, 32.9 percent; coal, 18.2 percent; hydro, 4.1 percent; and nuclear, 0.6 percent.[19] In 1971, 83 percent of the *electrical* energy used in the United States was produced from fossil fuel. Fifteen percent came from hydroelectric plants and the balance of 2 percent was produced by nuclear power.[20] Few, if any, good unoccupied sites remain available for dams for hydroelectric plants. Hydro-generating capacity will increase slowly or remain constant, but it will be a decreasing percentage of total electricity generated in the United States as the number of nonhydro plants increases.

It is claimed in the Federal Power Survey that by 1980 nuclear plants will be generating 22 percent of the nation's electricity, fossil fuel will provide 64 percent, and hydroelectric plants will produce 14 percent of the total.[21]

Effects of Bigness on Competitors

Besides making a system more vulnerable, bigness and its attendant uniformity discourage the use of nonuniform and often competitive resources. As a result, readily available sources of material or energy whose use could enhance the diversity of a system are virtually ignored. The allocation of funds in the federal budget for research and development shows that sources of energy other than nuclear and fossil fuel have not been seriously considered.

Budget figures for major federal energy research and development programs in 1973 and 1974[22] were as follows:

	1973 Appropriation	1974 Request
	(in millions)	
Nuclear	400.0	506.4
Coal	51.1	61.6
Oil and gas	23.2	23.4
Solar energy	4.0	12.0
Geothermal steam	4.1	4.0
Energy transmission and storage	2.5	3.0
Isotopes development	5.9	25.0

Nuclear power research and development was supported by more than 80 percent of the 1973 budget while solar and geothermal power each received less than 1 percent. However, as the following discussion will show, geothermal, solar, and other alternative systems have considerable promise and should be receiving a much larger share of government research and development funds.

Alternative Sources of Energy

Geothermal Energy

The basis of geothermal energy is hot underground rock in contact with water. The water is heated by the rock and the steam which is produced is captured and used for space heating or generating electricity in steam turbines. Natural geothermal sources have been used successfully for production of electricity in Italy since 1904.[23] In 1972 the worldwide productive capacity was 790.8 megawatts (MW) in seven countries, about 0.8 percent of total world electric generating capacity. The largest installation was Larderello Field in Italy, producing 358.6 MW. In the United States the only producing field was The Geysers in California, which had a capacity of 192 MW with additional capacity of 220 MW under construction.[24]

Steam can be secured by harnessing natural fumaroles or by drilling into underground areas of hot water and steam. It can also be produced by drilling two parallel holes into dry hot rock, fracturing the area at the bottom to join the two holes and then pumping water down one hole and capturing steam from the other.

There is great variation in predictions of the amount of electricity that can be generated from geothermal sources. The New Energy Forms Task Group of the National Petroleum Council in 1972 predicted that tapping steam and hot water deposits could provide energy to generate 7,000 to 19,000 MW by 1985.[25] The Panel on Geothermal Energy Resources of the Department of the Interior in its *Assessment of Geothermal Energy Resources* in 1972 estimated that with present technology, at least 19,000 MW of geothermal generating capacity could be installed by 1985. They estimated that 75,000 MW could be available by the year 2000. The panel suggested that with a modest research and development program, the generating capacity could be raised to 132,000 MW by 1985 and 395,000 MW by 2000.[26]

Walter Hickel as Chairman of the Geothermal Resources Research Conference stated:

> It would be a mistake, however, to look to electric power alone as the sole benefit from this unusual resource. . . . By 1985 we expect geothermal resources to provide up to 31.5 million acre feet of water to augment our national supplies. And geopressured reservoirs in the Gulf of Mexico will extract . . . perhaps a million standard cubic feet of natural gas per day per well.

Direct use of the heat itself will also be a valuable application. This will include the heating and cooling of residential and commercial buildings, as well as uses for farming and paper and pulp manufacturing.[27]

A final factor in favor of geothermal energy is the estimate that geothermal power plants can be built in less time than more conventional power plants.

> . . . geothermal plants should be operative in about two years, whereas fossil fuel power plants may require up to five years and nuclear plants up to ten.[28]

However, geothermal energy is not without its environmental impacts.[29] Highly mineralized waters from geothermal wells must be disposed of in such a way that ground and surface waters are not contaminated. It has been suggested that by re-injecting these brackish waters back into the earth, not only will the disposal problem be solved, but the occurrence of yet another undesirable side-effect — land subsidence over geothermal reservoirs — will be avoided. Air pollution is also a geothermal problem since many natural stream sources contain significant amounts of sulfur gases. None of these obstacles are insurmountable, however, and, in specific areas of the country, geothermal wells have the potential for becoming important energy supplements.

Solar Energy

Solar energy, a nonpolluting form of energy, has been used by man for centuries for drying food and for producing salt by evaporating salt water. At present it is also being used in some countries for space heating, water heating, and the desalinization of water. In a very limited way, primarily in the space program, it is being converted to electricity through photovoltaic cells, and research is being done on the large-scale production of electricity by steam turbine using solar heat.[30]

Enough is known about space and water heating so that it could be in much wider use in this country. The basic solar unit for space and water heating consists of a black plate which absorbs heat from the sun and transfers that heat to a water supply. In a space heating system, the heated water is circulated through radiators, and excess heat, in sufficient quantity to provide warmth through the night, is stored as hot water or heated gravel. Ordinarily a heating unit using electricity or fossil fuel is needed as a back-up system for use on cloudy days.

Solar water heating is an established business in Australia with production amounting to a million dollars annually. Solar water heaters are used routinely in homes and small commercial establishments, and are installed in all government houses. In Japan hundreds of thousands have been manufactured.[31] A few have been in use for many years in Florida, but they have seen little use elsewhere in the United States.

An increasing number of scientists are doing research on uses of solar energy.

> Within 5 years, many of these scientists believe, solar-powered systems for heating and cooling homes could be commercially available at prices competitive with gas or oil furnaces and electric air conditioners. . . . Substantial technical

problems remain to be solved in the design of cooling systems, in the manufacture of surface coatings for improved solar collectors, and in the optimization of combined solar heating and cooling systems. In most regions of the country back-up systems based on conventional fuels will be needed for extended periods of bad weather. Nonetheless, one estimate indicates that if systems were commercially available now, solar heating would be cheaper than electric heating in nearly all of the United States and would be competitive with gas and oil heating when these fuels double in cost. [R. Tybout and G. Lof, *Natur. Resour. J.* 10: 268 (1970).] Proponents believe that solar heating and cooling systems could ultimately supply as much as half of the nearly 20 percent of total U.S. energy consumption that is now used for residential and commercial space conditioning and could reduce the peak use of electricity in the summer.[32]

In 1973 less than 1 percent of federal support for energy research was allocated to solar energy development.[33]

Wind Energy

Wind, a major source of nonpolluting power for man in the past, has been almost totally displaced. Few commercial sailing ships survived the first quarter of the twentieth century. Holland's windmills, which had ground the flour and pumped the water from behind the dikes as land was reclaimed from the sea, were largely replaced by electric pumps fed by fossil-fuel-powered generators. Except in the outlying pastures, most wind-driven pumps on U.S. farms were replaced by electric or internal combustion motors. Thousands of wind-driven generators of 1 kilowatt or less which had powered farms and rural homes were retired when electricity became available from public utilities.

The potential for reviving wind-powered electric generating systems for today's society has been demonstrated. Russia has experimented with and developed new uses for wind power. In 1931 a wind-powered electric generator with a 100-kilowatt capacity was built near Balaklava on the Karen Heights of the Crimea. It supplied current to the Sevastopol power system for ten years until its destruction during World War II. Experimental research in windmill design was conducted in Denmark during the latter part of the twentieth century and has received continued support.[34] Since 1957 a fully automated 200-kilowatt generator has been successfully operated near Gedser, Denmark.[35] In 1961 the Electricity Authority of France was experimenting with a 900-kilowatt power plant powered by a three-bladed propeller 30 meters in diameter.[36] Between 1941 and 1945, a 1,250-kilowatt wind-powered generator was operated periodically at Grandpa's Knob near Rutland, Vermont.[37]

Several scales of electric generation by wind power have been studied. They include (1) massive installations in areas of favorable wind conditions, (2) generators providing supplementary power and integrated into a system of hydro and steam generators, and (3) small generators providing supplementary or, when used with storage batteries or flywheels, total power for a farm or home.

No massive installations have been built. However, Danish engineers have argued that a network of wind-powered generators similar to the 200-kilowatt wind turbine near Gedser, Denmark, would provide a feasible major source of electricity for that country, and the construction of a network of thousands of wind turbines on the Great Plains of the United States has been recently proposed.[38]

The 1,250-kilowatt wind turbine at Grandpa's Knob fed its power into the lines of a public utility in Vermont and is the largest wind-powered generator that has been operated on that basis in the United States. A proposal to install six 1,500-kilowatt wind turbines in the Green Mountains was abandoned after a study in 1945 indicated that the high cost of the turbines would prevent their producing electricity at competitive rates.[39]

The limiting factors in the development of the use of wind in the generation of electricity have been annual mean wind speed, which in some locations is too low to provide a practical source of power, and the comparatively lower cost of generation of electricity by alternative methods.[40] As fossil fuel becomes less available and more expensive, and particularly if external costs become internalized, the cost disadvantages of wind turbines may disappear.

As the knowledge of wind patterns and characteristics has increased greatly in the last half century, it has been suggested that cargo ships can be built which would use wind as the only source of motive power. These ships could carry 6,000 to 7,000 tons of cargo between Europe and Australia in an average time which is only twice that of a modern diesel-powered vessel. If low power electric motors were used to trim the sails, no larger crew would be needed than on a modern powered ship. The total fuel consumed for all purposes on a trip from Europe to Australia would be approximately the same as that now consumed by a similar sized motor ship as it crosses the North Sea.[41]

Research and development on ways to use the wind's energy effectively are sorely needed. Wind power may never become a dominant energy supply, but it can meet specific energy needs under particular conditions. In this way wind power can help bu ld a diverse and stable energy system.

Fuel Cells

Fuel cells rely on a chemical process to convert fuel into electricity. A fuel cell power plant usually includes a reformer to change the fuel to a form the cell can utilize, and an inverter to change the direct current which is produced to alternating current of desired frequency and voltage. Research and experimentation is being conducted on at least three applications of fuel cells. They are (1) on-site conversion of natural gas to electricity for direct use in residences and small business, (2) 25 to 100 MW high-output plants for supplementing a central station, and (3) 10 to 200 KW low-output plants that can run unattended and supply reliable power to remote locations. Fuel cell use for central stations is also being investigated.

Fuel cell power plants of 12.5 KW which use natural gas for fuel have been tested at thirty-seven locations in Canada and the United States. It is claimed by TARGET (Team to Advance Research for Gas Energy Transformation) that a fuel cell power plant which makes the conversion from gas to electricity at the user site is 20 to 25 percent more efficient than the conventional system of using gas to power a steam turbine at a central station and then transmitting the electricity to the user.

Fuel cells have several advantages. By mere addition or subtraction of cells, the size of a generating unit can be changed. Air and noise pollution is negligible. The waste heat can be vented to the air and, in the case of small units located in residential and commercial buildings, can possibly be used for supplementary water heating, space heating, and air-conditioning.[42]

Maintaining Diversity

For the sake of stability, a diverse energy base is needed. Wherever a natural energy source is locally abundant its use should be encouraged. Thus we might soon have solar heating in general use in the southwest, wind-powered electric units on the high plains, and geothermal electric generation in fumarole areas and in those parts of the country where hot subsurface rock can be feasibly reached by drilling.

Each adds only a small portion of the total energy supply. But if small solar units and windmills were used only as supplements to conventional sources, they would greatly decrease the number of nuclear or fossil fuel generating plants needed within a region. Just as important is the fact that, as they ordinarily would produce energy at or near the place the energy was to be used, they would not add to the load on the electric transmission lines.

Even when we think we have found what we believe to be the best product or the best method or the best source of supply, we must continue to seek, develop, and use alternatives. With the passage of time, reliable methods become obsolete and reliable sources of supply become exhausted. Unless new methods and sources are developed, reliance is placed upon a decreasing number of alternatives and diversity is reduced.

Why do men seek new sources and develop new processes? The desire for profits has been, and continues to be, a driving force. Ironically, this short-term gain is also the driving force behind the quest for uniformity once a new process is found. Uniformity usually increases efficiency, increases production, and simplifies administration. The gains from diversity are more likely to be realized only in the future and their effects on the decision-maker are likely to be remote.

What procedures can be developed that will assure the continuing conception and proposal of reasonable alternatives? What incentives can be provided?

Several federal statutes require that alternatives be described or at least that alternatives be sought before a federal agency can approve or engage in certain specified types of activities.

The Federal Aid Highway Act (23 U.S.C. § 138) denies approval to "any program or project which requires the use of any publicly owned land from a public park, recreation area, or wildlife and waterfowl refuge. . . unless. . . there is no feasible and prudent alternative to the use of such land. . . ."

The National Environmental Policy Act, which became effective in early 1970, requires an environmental impact statement to be included by federal agencies in "every recommendation or report on proposals for legislation and other major Federal actions significantly affecting the quality of the human environment. . . ."[43] The impact statement must include a detailed statement of "alternatives to the proposed action."[44] Court decisions have emphasized the importance and necessity of including discussion of alternatives in impact statements.[45]

Occasionally legislative or administrative bodies create commissions or study groups to consider major policy questions and report their findings and recommendations to the body which appointed them. Examples of such groups at the congressional level are the Public Land Law Review Commission which reported to Congress in 1970[46] and the Materials Policy Commission which reported in 1973.[47] Sometimes the study groups are asked to make alternative, rather than single, recommendations.

Some agencies which are responsible for management of a resource also conduct research to diversify uses of the resource. For example, the United States Forest Service through its Forest Products Laboratory constantly seeks new ways to use and reuse timber. The United States Geological Survey conducts a continuous search for new sources of minerals.

Constant research and development are needed to find and expand uses for materials that are now disposed of as waste; to find substitutes for materials which are now in use; and to develop different manufacturing and refining processes. Research on resources, the results of which do not appear to offer immediate opportunity for use and profit, should not be neglected.

—Talent and training within research groups should be diverse. If research groups combine the diverse knowledge, insight, and approaches of people from different disciplines and backgrounds, new practical solutions to resource problems are more likely to be found than if the study involves only people from one discipline or several similar disciplines.

Researchers and decision-makers must always be aware that we as people and as a nation are weakened, rather than strengthened, if a single solution to a specific resource problem is adopted and universally implemented to the exclusion of all others. We must seek to broaden our base, not narrow it.

References

1. "Air Conditioners," *Consumer Reports*, July 1973, p. 443.
2. "Washing Machines," *Consumer Reports*, September 1972, p. 573.
3. "Dishwashers," *Consumer Reports*, November 1971, p. 660.
4. See also the discussion of energy efficiency in Chapter 7, above.
5. *Material Needs and the Environment, Today and Tomorrow*, National Commission on M terials Policy Final Report, (Washington, D.C.: 1973), pp. 1-5.
6. *Man, Materials and Environment*, Report by Study Committee on Environmental Aspects of a National Materials Policy, National Academy of Sciences (Washington, D.C.: 1973), p. 25.
7. *Bituminous Coal Facts, 1972*, National Coal Association (Washington, D.C.: 1972), pp. 14-16.
8. E. A. Nephew, "Healing Wounds," *Environment*, January-February 1972, p. 15.
9. *Genetic Vulnerability of Major Crops*, Committee on Genetic Vulnerability of Major Crops, National Research Council, National Academy of Sciences (Washington, D.C.: 1972), pp. 124, 135.

10. Ibid., p. 15.

11. Ibid., p. 127.

12. E. E. Saari, "Wheat Rusts in West Asia and North Africa and the Possibilities for Development of Resistant Varieties Through International Cooperation," *Proceedings of the European and Mediterranean Cereal Rusts Conference*, Prague, 1972, pp. 213-17; also, E. E. Saari and J. M. Prescott, "Identifying Sources of Rust Resistance Through International Testing," ibid., pp. 219-23.

13. *The International Rice Research Institute Annual Report for 1968*, (Los Banos, Philippines: 1968), pp. 79-85.

14. R. L. Doutt and R. F. Smith, "The Pesticide Syndrome — Diagnosis and Suggested Prophylaxis," in C. B. Huffaker, ed., *Biological Control*, (New York: Plenum Press, 1971), p. 3.

15. Ibid., p. 5.

16. Ibid., pp. 8-9.

17. R. Van den Bosch, T. F. Leigh, L. A. Falcon, V. M. Stern, D. Gonzales, and K. S. Hagen, "The Developing Programs of Integrated Control of Cotton Pests in California," in Huffaker, *Biological Control*, pp. 378-82; see also *Integrated Pest Management*, Report of Council on Environmental Quality (Washington, D.C.: U.S. Government Printing Office, 1972), pp. 9-30. R. F. Smith and R. Van den Bosch, "Integrated Control," in W. W. Kilgore and R. L. Doutt, eds., *Pest Control: Biological, Physical and Selected Chemical Methods* (New York: Academic Press, 1967), pp. 295-340.

18. William Longgood, *The Darkening Land* (New York: Simon & Schuster, 1972), p. 210.

19. *Energy Crisis in America*, Congressional Quarterly Inc., (Washington, D.C.: 1973), Figure 3, p. 5.

20. *1970 National Power Survey*, Report by the Federal Power Commission, 4 vols. (Washington, D.C.: U.S. Government Printing Office, 1971), vol. I, Table 1.3, p. 1-18.

21. Ibid.

22. Figures based on those published in *Conservation Foundation Letter*, February, 1973, p. 6.

23. *Assessment of Geothermal Energy Resources*, Panel on Geothermal Resources, U.S. Department of Interior (Washington, D.C.: 1972), p. 22.

24. Ibid.

25. Ibid., p. 85.

26. Ibid., p. 4.

27. Walter J. Hickel, *Geothermal Energy*, Final Report of the Geothermal Resources Research Conference, Battelle Seattle Research Center, Seattle, Washington, September 18-20, 1972 (University of Alaska, 1972), pp. iii-iv.

28. Ibid., p. 6.

29. "Geothermal Energy: An Emerging Major Resource," *Science* 177:980 (September 15, 1972).

30. *Solar Energy in Developing Countries: Perspectives and Prospects*, National Academy of Sciences (Washington, D.C.: 1972), pp. 2-3.

31. Ibid., pp. 16-17.

32. Allen L. Hammond, "Solar Energy: the Largest Resource," *Science*, 177: 1088 (September 22, 1972); statement as to comparative costs is also supported by H. C. Hottel; and J. B. Howard, *New Energy Technology — Some Facts and Assessments* (Cambridge, Mass.: MIT Press, 1971).

33. See figures on p. 123 above, and note 20.

34. E. W. Golding, *The Generation of Electricity by Wind Power* (London: E. and F. N. Spon, 1955), pp. 15-16.

35. Julian McCaull, "Windmills," *Environment*, January-February 1973, p. 15.

36. P. Ailleret, "The Abundance of Natural Energy and the Choice of the Means of Harnessing It," *Proceedings of the United Nations Conference on New Sources of Energy, Solar Energy, Wind Power, and Geothermal Energy*, 1961, vol. 1, General Sessions (Rome: 1961), p. 33.

37. McCaull, "Windmills," p. 7.

38. Ibid., pp. 7,15.

39. Ibid., pp. 11-12.

40. Golding, *Generation of Electricity by Wind*, p. 38.

41. Basil Greenhill, "The Sailing Ship in a Fuel Crisis," *Ecologist*, vol. 2, no. 9, p. 9 (September 1972).

42. Thomas H. Maugh, II, "Fuel Cells: Dispersed Generation of Electricity," *Science* 178:1274-1274a (December 22, 1972).

43. National Environmental Policy Act, §102, 42 U.S.C. § 4332 (1970).

44. Ibid.

45. J. MacDonald and J. Conway, *Environmental Litigation,* University of Wisconsin Extension Department of Law (Madison: 1972) pp. 163-73; *Environmental Quality, 1972,* Third Annual Report of the Council on Environmental Quality (Washington, D.C.: 1972), p. 243.

46. *One Third of the Nation's Land,* Report of the Public Land Law Review Commission (Washington, D.C.: 1970).

47. *Material Needs and the Environment, Today and Tomorrow,* National Commission on Materials Policy Final Report (Washington, D.C.: 1973).

9.   Small Steps to Solve Big Problems

Major change for the better can seldom if ever be accomplished by one law or decision or discovery. Though major goals may be simply described, such as energy conservation or clean air, a multitude of small steps must be taken over a period of time if such a goal is to be accomplished.

The Incremental Effect

The present pollution of much of our air and water and the shortages of desired materials did not occur because of a single decision or a few activities. Our present patterns of land use were established over decades and centuries and are based on the desires and activities of generations of people. Numerous negative increments were needed to produce the kind of pollution seen in the Cuyahoga River of Ohio which caught fire in 1969,[1] or that seen in a 12-mile-diameter area in the Atlantic Ocean off New York City where bacteriological contamination is so extensive that shell fishing has been prohibited.[2] There are other examples of extensive pollution: the amount of oil spilled annually into the sea between 1970 and 1973 is equal to half the total quantity dispersed into the oceans from sunken tankers during the six years of World War II;[3] samples taken during 1972 by marine research vessels of the National Oceanic and Atmospheric Administration revealed that over half of the plankton collected in a survey from Cape Cod to the Caribbean Sea was contaminated with oil. One research ship, the *Albatross IV*, reported that its collecting nets had been fouled by oil clumps 75 percent of the time.[4]

Numerous man-made negative increments also have brought about untimely climatic change. Uncontrolled emissions from manufacturing and refining processes and the burning of fossil fuel have increased both the carbon dioxide and particulate matter content of the atmosphere. An increased percentage of carbon dioxide in the air can raise the temperature of the atmosphere by reducing reradiation of heat from the earth back into space.[5] On the other hand, increased particulate matter in the air can cool the earth's atmosphere by reflecting back into space too much of the incident energy from the sun.[6]

Geologists believe that temperature fluctuations of no more than six degrees centigrade accompanied the great climatic changes of the glacial Pleistocene epoch.[7] While conclusive evidence is lacking, it is claimed that increased carbon dioxide and particulate levels in our present atmosphere have simultaneously raised tempera- tures in the equatorial regions and lowered them in the polar regions, resulting in a changing global weather pattern.[8] Similarly, industrial man's city has created its own high-temperature microclimate by trapping both natural and man-made heat within its concrete canyons and under its smoggy roof.[9]

Such large scale pollutions may be natural outcomes of the fact that, with the technology prevalent in industrialized society today, materials processing, fuel transport, and power generation increase as world population increases. But while it is logical to expect polluting residuals to accompany these processes, it does not necessarily follow that pollution is inevitable and environmental damage is unavoidable.

Under public pressure, governments and industries have acknowledged, often grudgingly, that there *are* ways to "defuse" potential pollutants and recycle them into useful products. But to actually change longstanding industrial practices or individual habits, or to break down the economic barriers to pollution control and recycling is a difficult task. It is also a task that demands "thinking small" since the possibilities of finding a solution or implementing a change increase with the number of small coordinated actions that are recognized and taken. Seeking big, one-step solutions to complex problems is a waste of valuable time. Before any major change can be achieved, separate remedies must be sought for the separate facets of a problem. These remedies may include changes in equipment, methods, attitudes, and rules.

A Case in Point: Reduction of Pollution from Stack Emissions

As an example of a complex problem and the many components of its solution, let us consider pollution caused by stack emissions from a steam turbine electric generating plant which uses coal as its source of heat. The common stack emissions considered to be harmful are particulate matter, generally referred to as fly ash, and sulfur gas, ordinarily in the form of SO_2

Most coals contain a significant percentage of fly ash. A witness testifying on electrical power production in the Southwest suggested that a 5,000 megawatt generating complex fired with Utah coal and operating at an 0.6 load factor (the average generation as a fraction of total capacity) would require approximately 1,000 tons of coal per hour.[10] This would produce approximately 80 tons of ash per hour, of which approximately 63 tons would go up the stack.[11]

The sulfur content of coal is measured in terms of pounds of sulfur oxides per million BTUs of heat generated by the coal. If coal combustion produces more than 1.2 pounds of sulfur oxides per million BTUs of heat generated, a coal-burning power plant with uncontrolled emissions will not satisfy the 1975 performance standards set by the Environmental Protection Agency for new power plants.[12] According to the National Coal Association (NCA), meeting these standards without emission control equipment would require a sulfur content of no more than

0.7 percent for the average coal mined east of the Mississippi River, and an even lower sulfur content for western coals because of their lower BTU rating.[13] The NCA claims that only 14.4 percent of the domestic bituminous coal, which constitutes about one-half of the total coal supply, contains sulfur in concentrations of 0.7 percent or less.[14]

A simplistic solution to the problem of sulfur in stack emissions is to stipulate that only low sulfur coal be burned. Both particulate matter and sulfur gas could be virtually eliminated from stack emissions by completely prohibiting coal fuel and requiring that coal burning furnaces be converted to low sulfur fuel oil or gas-burning furnaces. New York City is trying this approach and, since 1966, has progressively reduced the legally permissible sulfur content of fuels stored or burned within the city.[15] If legislation requiring such a change were adopted and enforced nationally, certain stack emissions might conceivably be temporarily alleviated. But such action also would create other major problems, primarily fuel shortages and misallocations of fuel supplies.

To refrain from using coal, America's currently most abundant source of energy, because of unsolved stack emission problems appears to be shortsighted policy in both national and international terms. Approximately 1600 billion tons of coal are available in the United States using present mining methods.[16] This would last for at least 3,200 years at the present production rate of approximately 0.5 billion tons per year,[17] and would reduce some of the need to import other fuels during that period. At present we are importing both petroleum and natural gas to meet current fuel demand, and the amount we import is increasing each year. Thus coal will continue as a major energy source for at least the immediate future, because alternative fuel supplies are insufficient.

For this reason it would be wise national policy to use high sulfur coal in all major energy-demanding installations such as electric generating plants, provided that incentives are created for sulfur removal, coal gasification, or other appropriate measures to minimize pollution. Low sulfur coal then could be reserved for the many smaller users who would find purchase of sulfur removal equipment prohibitively expensive.

The major goal in reducing stack emissions is to enable continued production of large quantities of electrical energy from fossil fuels while reducing damage to the environment. An equally important goal should be to increase use of that domestic fuel which is in greatest supply, coal. By using more coal, we avoid premature exhaustion of other fuels and retain a diversity of fuels for the future. Increased use of coal, in turn, suggests the need to find economic uses for coal's residual materials which would otherwise require disposal as solid or liquid waste.

The following discussion presents an array of individual steps which could be taken to accomplish these goals and keep new problems to a minimum.

(1) Legislation Requiring Reduced Pollution. Existing legislation could be implemented and additional legislation could be adopted to require reduction of known pollutants from stack emissions. In addition to ambient air standards, emission standards could be set for both particulate matter and sulfur.[18]

Equipment to constantly monitor and report the extent to which these substances are present in the stack gas could be required. These requirements have been implemented for new stationary sources through the Environmental Protection Agency under the present Clean Air Act.[19] Enforcement is accomplished by enacting penalities against those who knowingly violate provisions of the act.[20] Consideration could be given to adoption of new legislation at both federal and state levels providing for emission permits and effluent charges,[21] two somewhat controversial approaches. The emission permit authorizes some air pollution, but limits its extent, and the effluent charge requires the polluter to pay for his pollution.

More could be done also to control emissions at major sources such as coal-fired power plants. At present, states which regulate the price at which electricity is sold to consumers require that all reasonable capital expenditures for electric generating equipment be included in the rate base. Appropriate legislation should be adopted where needed to include in the rate base reasonable expenditures for pollution reduction equipment.

(2) Installation of Sulfur Removal Equipment.   There is currently a need for both better design in sulfur removal equipment and more willingness on the part of sulfur emitters to try various combinations of sulfur removal strategies.

A major obstacle to sulfur removal is that equipment which will effectively remove SO_2 from the stack gases of one industry will not necessarily be efficient when applied to the stacks of a different industry. Each method of SO_2 removal is designed to handle a specific combination of gas temperatures, concentration of SO_2, and concentration of other gases and particulate matter.

Several methods have been developed for the removal of sulfur gas from copper smelter emissions. The four most important processes, all of which recover the sulfur in a saleable form, such as pure sulfur or sulfuric acid, are as follows:[22]

Monsanto Cat-Ox Process is adapted from the sulfuric acid contact process and is particularly suitable for emissions which have a low percent of sulfur gas.

Wellman-Power Gas Process uses sodium sulfite solution as the SO_2 absorbent in cyclic absorption-desorption.

Allied SO_2 Process uses natural gas (methane) as a reductant in the direct catalytic reduction of SO_2 to sulfur. This method requires a relatively high percentage of SO in the emission stream. It can be used as a second stage process to produce elemental sulfur from the concentrated SO_2 stream produced by another process such as the Wellman-Power Gas.

Bureau of Mines Citrate Process uses a partially neutralized solution of citric acid as the absorbent and then uses hydrogen sulfide to secure elemental sulfur.

The Monsanto Cat-Ox Process, the Wellman Power Gas Process, and other SO_2 removal systems have been used experimentally at electric generating plants[23] as well as at copper smelters. But nowhere in the United States is this equipment installed at any coal-burning electric generating plant other than on an experimental or pilot project basis. The official industry position is that there is as yet no sulfur removal equipment available which is adequate for use in a fossil fuel generating plant.[24]

According to the spokesmen for the power industry, the major issue is the reliability of the removal equipment. Because the industry must produce power continuously, the amount of stand-by generating capacity that any power network must maintain is affected by the reliability of the generating plants in the system. The utility operators emphasize that they must avoid any type of equipment which, because of its need for periodic service or repair, may increase the time during which a generating plant is out of service. In addition, sulfur removal equipment is expensive and requires skilled operators. The industry does not presently recognize any sulfur removal process as sufficiently reliable.[25]

The industry position is that until acceptable sulfur removal equipment is available, the potential air pollution from high sulfur fuels can be handled by building higher stacks.[26] With stacks of 100 or more feet, it is argued that the sulfur is dispersed over a wider area, its concentration is diluted, and harmful effects are reduced.[27]

Opponents of this view argue that dilution by tall stacks is possible only if the ambient air does not already contain sulfur gas from other sources. Furthermore, there is evidence that in at least some geographical locations and under some conditions the high stack cannot disperse the sulfur gas sufficiently to prevent its combining with water in the atmosphere to form sulfuric acid. The acid falls to the ground in sulfuric-acid-enriched rain.[28] The only change resulting from the use of the higher stack may be that the acid-enriched rain falls farther from the plant than would be the case with a shorter stack.[29]

Regardless of how effective the high stack may be in reducing the concentration of sulfur gas in the ambient air, it is obvious that it does nothing to recover the sulfur. The sulfur is so dispersed that it is not feasible to ever recapture it commercially.

However, if a high stack were used as a back-up for a sulfur removal system, power plants could continue operating despite a breakdown in equipment. When the removal equipment of the regular stack was not functioning properly, the emissions could be diverted through additional heaters to the high stack and dispersed until repairs could be made. Installing sulfur removal equipment and a high stack as a back-up would be one means of allowing the electric industry to continue using coal as an energy source, eliminate air pollution, and recover sulfur for industrial use.

(3) Development of a Market for Recovered Sulfur and Cutting of Subsidies to Sulfur Mines.   If sulfur gas is removed from the stack and converted to sulfuric acid or elemental sulfur, what is to be done with it? Elemental sulfur can be converted to sulfuric acid and vice versa; but is there a market for either product or must they be disposed of as solid or liquid waste? Power companies claim that with present acid prices and transport costs, they cannot afford to store recovered sulfuric acid or ship it to a potential user.[30] Unless suitable markets for sulfur are nearby, it is reportedly cheaper to bury the sulfur sludge than to reclaim it as elemental sulfur.[31]

A question that must be answered is whether, as a nation, we can afford not to use the recoverable sulfur. Nearly 10 million long tons of sulfur were consumed in the

TABLE 9.1.   Sulfur Resources of the United States (in millions of long tons)

	Identified	Hypothetical	Speculative	Total
Elemental sulfur deposits in evaporites	200	100	150	450
Hydrogen sulfide in sour natural gas	15	185	—	200
Organic sulfur in petroleum	255	1,000	—	1,255
Pyrite deposits	100	20	20	140
Elemental sulfur in volcanic rocks	30	+	+	30
Sulfur contained in metallic sulfides	100	100	200	400
Gypsum	7,200	1,800	—	9,000
Organic sulfur in pyrites and coals	21,400	19,600	—	41,000
Organic sulfur in tar sands	10	—	—	10
Organic sulfur and pyrites in oil shale and shale rich in organic matter	+	+	—	81,000
Total	29,310	22,805	370	133,485

+ some resources but amount not estimated
Source: Brobst and Pratt, *U.S. Mineral Resources,* Table 126, p. 613.

United States in 1970. While there are several sources of sulfur as industrial by-products in the United States (Table 9.1), 75 percent of 1970 consumption, 7.5 million tons, came from twelve elemental sulfur mines on the Gulf Coast and in West Texas.[32] This tonnage amounts to 5 percent of our present identified recoverable elemental sulfur deposits. It is predicted that consumption will increase by 4 or 5 percent per year and will be 30 million tons annually by 2000.[33]

It is significant that in the United States in the early 1970s each 1,000 megawatt power plant which burned high sulfur coal dispersed approximately 89,000 tons of sulfur, in the form of sulfur dioxide, into the atmosphere.[34] In 1969, the total of these emissions was 7 million tons of sulfur, an amount almost equal to the tonnage of sulfur taken from Texas mines in 1970 (see above).[35]

It is unlikely that recovered sulfur will become competitive with mined elemental sulfur as long as the federal government pursues its present policy of subsidizing elemental sulfur mines. This subsidization is being done as follows:

1. For income tax purposes, there is a depletion allowance of 22 percent for the mining of elemental sulfur in domestic and foreign mines. Several

other minerals have an equally high depletion allowance but none have one which is higher, and uranium is the only other hard-rock mineral to be granted a depletion allowance for foreign deposits.[36]

2. There is eligibility for federal loans for up to 50 percent of the exploration costs.[37]

3 For income tax purposes, the right is granted to deduct exploration costs as expenses rather than to capitalize the cost.[38]

In the light of current sulfur dioxide removal and disposal problems, these subsidies to sulfur mines are questionable and the existing federal statutes should be amended or repealed to eliminate them.

(4) Legislation to Increase the Market for Fly Ash. Unlike the continuing problem of sulfur dioxide emissions, the problem of capturing particulate matter from stack gases has been largely solved. Known as fly ash, the particulates from coal-fired power plants can be recovered with the use of electrostatic precipitators. Most precipitators can remove 90 percent of the fly ash from an airstream. The remaining 10 percent can be almost entirely removed by running the airstream through a bag house or additional precipitator units.[39] Unfortunately, the particles that are most damaging to human health (0.5 to 2.0 microns in size) are also the most difficult to remove from a gas stream. Generally, equipment that is efficient enough to capture these particles is very expensive to operate.[40]

With dependable precipitators in general use nationwide, the critical question has been how to utilize the 40 million tons of fly ash which they capture annually.[41] Fly ash has been used to some extent for years as a partial substitute for cement in the making of concrete. The resultant concrete is as good as non-fly ash concrete from every standpoint except for strength during the period of hardening, and is better in its plasticity and in its resistance to water and mild acids.[42]

It could be reasonable national policy to encourage use of fly ash, which otherwise has to be disposed of as solid waste, as a substitute for part of cement, a material which requires energy and virgin resources for its manufacture. The federal government could even require maximum use of fly ash in the construction of all concrete highways which are supported in whole or in part with federal funds, and in all structures which are federally owned or are paid for in whole or in part through the use of federal funds.

(5) Legislation for Rehabilitation of Land After Strip Mining. Besides the objections to coal fuel as a source of air pollution, there is also objection to its use because of the tremendous economic and environmental losses incurred in regions where coal is strip mined. But rather than an outright ban on the stripping of coal, state and federal legislation is needed to assure that regardless of who has title to the land, the surface will be restored as part of the cost of mining as soon as the coal has been removed. If the land is of such slope or texture that it cannot be restored or improved, strip mining should be carefully balanced against the permanent loss of that land for other purposes.[43] Laws that require licenses for mine operators, that grant mining permits only after presentation and approval of plans for each mine operation, and that require the posting of a bond to guarantee reclamation performance already have been adopted by some states[44] and are under consideration by Congress.[45] When laws are effective and mine operators are interested, results have been somewhat encouraging.

These five steps — legislation to tighten emission standards, design and installation of efficient and reliable sulfur removal systems on stacks, creation of a market for recovered sulfur by eliminating subsidies to mined sulfur, specification of fly ash cement in federal or state funded concrete construction projects, and tighter controls on strip mining and land reclamation — suggest a basic strategy for making America's vast coal supplies a blessing rather than a problem.

This is not to say that each step, because it is small, will be easy. Achieving *any* change in the status quo requires dogged determination and perseverance. The important point is that the solution of a complex problem is almost of necessity complex. Many small increments or changes are needed to achieve a big change.

References

1. Don Widener, *Timetable for Disaster* (Los Angeles: Nash Publications, 1970), p. 170.
2. *Ocean Dumping: A National Policy Report to the President,* prepared by the Council on Environmental Quality (Washington, D.C.: Government Printing Office, 1970), p. 16.
3. Roger Revelle, Edward Wenk, Bostwick H. Ketchum, and Edward R. Corino, "Ocean Pollution by Petroleum Hydrocarbons," in William H. Matthews, ed., *Man's Impact on Terrestrial and Oceanic Ecosystems* (Cambridge, Mass.: MIT Press, 1971), p. 303.
4. United States Department of Commerce, National Oceanic and Atmospheric Administration, Release No. NOAA 73-17, February 13, 1973.
5. Helmut E. Landsberg, "Man-Made Climatic Changes," *Science,* 170:1266-67 (December 18, 1970).
6. Reid A. Bryson and Wayne M. Wendland, "Climatic Effects of Atmospheric Pollution," in S. Fred Singer, ed., *Global Effects of Environmental Pollution* (New York: Springer-Verlag, 1970), p. 134.
7. Richard F. Flint, *Glacial and Pleistocene Geology* (New York: John Wiley and Sons, 1957), p. 487.
8. Reid A. Bryson, "Drought in Sahelia," *The Ecologist* 3:369-70 (October 1973).
9. James T. Peterson, "Climate of the City," in Thomas R. Detwyler, ed., *Man's Impact on Environment* (New York: McGraw-Hill, 1971), pp. 133-39.
10. Malcolm F. Baldwin, *The Southwest Energy Complex: A Policy Evaluation,* The Conservation Foundation (Washington, D.C.: 1973), p. 17.
11. U.S., Congress, Senate, Committee on Interior and Insular Affairs, "Problems of Electrical Power Production in the Southwest," Part 3: Hearings, Statement by Dr. Noel de Nevers, 92nd Congress, 1st session, May 26, 1971, pp. 1020-40.
12. 40 CFR § 60.43 (1972).
13. *Bituminous Coal Facts, 1972,* National Coal Association (Washington, D.C.: 1972), p. 8.

14. Ibid., p. 75. The same table also reports that 66 percent of subbituminous coal and 77 percent of the lignite reserves contain 0.7 percent or less sulfur, but because of the lower BTU output of these types of coal, these figures do not represent the actual amounts which could be burned without emission controls.

15. New York, N.Y., 1969 Amendment to Local Law No. 14, 893-1.0 (1966).

16. *Bituminous Coal Facts, 1972*, p. 9. (Extracted from Paul Averitt, "Coal Resources of the United States, January 1, 1967," U.S. Geological Survey Bulletin 1275, 1969.).

17. Ibid., p. 11.

18. *Ambient standards* refer to the quantity of pollutant which is permitted in the free air in the locality of the source of emission. *Emission standards* refer to the quantity of pollutant which may be emitted by a specific source of emission. In terms of equity, feasibility of enforcement, and effectiveness in pollution control, the two types of standards differ considerably.

19. Clean Air Act, 42 U.S.C. §§ 1857c-6, 1857c-9(a) (1970); 40CFR §§ 60.40-.46 (1972).

20. Clean Air Act, 42 U.S.C. §§ 1857c-8(c) (1970), *as amended*, (Supp. I, 1971).

21. *Pollution permits* establish maximum quantities of pollutant which may be legally emitted by a specific source. *Effluent charges* are charges assessed against one who emits pollutants. The charges increase as the quantity of emissions increases. The charge can be based on the cost to remove the pollutant or on the deleterious effects of the pollutant on the environment.

22. "Cleaning up SO₂," *Engineering and Mining Journal* combined with *Chemical Engineering,* April 1973, pp. AAA-CCC.

23. *Bituminous Coal Facts, 1972,* pp. 24-24; Alfred J. Van Tassel, ed., *Environmental Side Effects of Rising Industrial Output* (Lexington, Mass.: Heath, 1970), pp. 177-81; and statement to Leonardo Seminar by Sol Burstein, Senior Vice President, Wisconsin Electric Power Co., April 11, 1973.

24. *Bituminous Coal Facts, 1972,* p. 23; A. V. Slack and H. L. Falkenberry, "SO₂: More Questions than Answers," *Electrical World,* December 15, 1971, pp. 50-51.

25. "Air Quality: A Continuing Effort — and a Continuing Problem," *Edison Electric Institute Bulletin,* September-October 1973, pp. 210-11; and *Energy Policy Statement,* Edison Electric Institute (New York: 1972), p. 7.

26. Statement to Leonardo Seminar by W. Dunham Crawford, president, Edison Electric Institute, May 8, 1973.

27. Norman Wesler, "Air Pollution and the Projected Consumption of Fossil Fuels for Purposes Other than Internal Combustion Engines," in Alfred J. Van Tassel, *Environmental Side Effects of Rising Industrial Output,* pp. 182-84.

28. See discussions in Gene E. Likens, "Acid Rain," *Environment,* March 1972, pp. 33-40, and Arild Holt-Jensen, "Acid Rains in Scandinavia," *Ecologist,* vol. 3, no. 10 (October 1973), pp. 378-82.

29. Erik Eriksson, "The Fate of SO₂ and NOₓ in the Atmosphere," in David A. Berkowitz and Arthur M. Squires, eds., *Power Generation and Environmental Change* (Cambridge, Mass.: MIT Press, 1971) pp. 297-99.

30. Final Report of Sulfur Oxide Control Technology Assessment Panel (SOCTAP) on Projected Utilization of Stack Gas Cleaning Systems by Steam Electric Plants, submitted to Federal Interagency Committee Evaluation of State Air Implementation plans, April 15, 1973, p. 57.

31. Ibid., pp. 57-58.

32.   A. J. Bodenlos, "Sulfur," in D. A. Brobst, and W. P. Pratt, *United States Mineral Resources* (Washington, D.C.: Government Printing Office, 1973), p. 610.

33.   Ibid., p. 606

34.   SOCTAP Report, p. 53.

35.   Arthur M. Squires, "Clean Power from Coal at a Profit," in Berkowitz and Squires, *Power Generation and Environmental Change*, p. 175.

36.   Internal Revenue Code of 1954, § 613 (b).

37.   30 U.S.C. § 641-646 (1970).

38.   Internal Revenue Code of 1954, § 617.

39.   U.S., Congress, Senate, Committee on Interior and Insular Affairs, "Problems of Electrical Power Production in the Southwest," Part 3: Hearings, Statement by Dr. Noel de Nevers, 92nd Congress, 1st Session, May 26, 1971, p. 1024.

40.   Harold E. Hesketh, *Understanding and Controlling Air Pollution* (Ann Arbor, Mich.: Ann Arbor Science Publishers, Inc., 1973), pp. 3, 359.

41.   Frank J. Quilici, *Characteristics and Uses of Montana Fly Ash,* Montana Bureau of Mines and Geology Bulletin 90, (Butte, Montana: Montana College of Mineral Science and Technology, September 1973), p. 1.

42.   Ibid., pp. 5-7.

43.   See discussion of the potential loss of food-producing capacity due to strip mining in Chapter 6, above.

44.   E.g., Ky. Rev. Stat, §§ 350.010-.240 (1970), *as amended,* (Cum. Supp. 1972); Rev. Codes of Mont. Ann., SS 50-1018 to -1033 (Supp. 1971); West Virginia Code §§ 20-6-32 (1970).

45.   Senate Hearings before Committee on Interior and Insular Affairs on S. 425 and S. 923, March, 1973.

10.   Can There Be Equity?

As we noted in Chapter 1, exponential increases in the rate of resource consumption, as reflected by the increases in the GNP (see Table 1.2 of that chapter), cannot continue indefinitely. In formulating resource policy for the future, there is a very real need to inquire into what can be done to achieve a better life for mankind now and in the future without going to rates of resource consumption — such as a worldwide application of the U.S. lifestyle might bring about — that cannot be sustained.

Ideal Survival

The above line of inquiry leads to a concept that may be called "ideal survival." For the time being it is not important to define "ideal survival" in an absolute sense, but rather to consider how to eliminate, as much as possible, the causes of "miserable survival." Thus, in an approach that can be described as "going in the back door," we can define "ideal survival" as a way of life in which attempts to improve living conditions are more substantial than at present.

A new science that may bring us closer to ideal survival in the future is biocybernetics, the science of survival-oriented communication and regulation through feedback in organized biological systems. A simple example of feedback regulation is the home thermostat, in which rising temperature activates a switch that shuts off the heating unit when the desired temperature has been reached and turns it on when the temperature falls below that level. A humanistically guided biocybernetic technology could be used not only to detect, measure, and communicate information about the successes of social interventions (laws, inventions, technologies), but also to provide early warnings about their undesirable and unintended consequences.[1]

Biocybernetic technology relies on *indicators* that reflect the status of the society as a whole. GNP may be a good economic indicator but, as it stands, it is inadequate as a national index of well-being. A biocybernetic technology based on the concept of ideal survival must seek out *social indicators* which, like the GNP, "aggregate observations in limited areas by various means,"[2] but, unlike the GNP, put the emphasis on criteria of physical and mental health. These indicators would define trends in such things as infant mortality, communicable disease, causes of death, and malnutrition and relate them to attempts to diminish "miserable survival."

We would expect such a technology to measure social indicators on a continuing basis and to transmit the information to the public and to decision-makers. The results of the decision-makers' actions could be judged then by further changes in the social indicators.

An adequate biocybernetic technology would be one that meets the functional needs of society while maintaining individual and cultural diversity. It would also maintain a healthy respect for man's unpredictability as well as for his values and ethical considerations.[3] Such a system would require a distribution of powers and responsibilities that would prevent the emergence of a single controlling "priesthood" (see Chapter 5 above, p. 65).

Human misery will always be present despite our best efforts, yet that should not deter us from attempting to achieve ideal survival. We emphasize here that the goal is not uniformity or homogeneity of human existence. Alleviation of human misery does not have to be at the expense of cultural diversity or of individual development and happiness.

Can There Be Equity?

In a world in which the gross national product per capita (GNPPC) varies from a low of less than $100 per year in many African countries and about $100 per year in India and Pakistan to a high of $4,240 per year (United States 1972),[4] the problem of equitable resource distribution looms large. The GNP, which already is highly correlated with what may be called "resource consumption," needs to be examined for further correlation with various indices of national or global welfare. In the meantime, present GNP can be compared with available social indicators such as infant mortality to give some idea of the problem of equity.

Figure 10.1 shows a correlation between IM or infant mortality (here defined as the percent of infants that die in the first year after birth), the GNPPC, and the birth rate. It is clear that increases in GNPPC were *not* correlated with a further lowering in IM after reaching $1,500. On the other hand, high birth rates correlate with high IM, and both correlate with low GNPPC. Even with a high rate of IM, the extremely high birth rates lead to a high net increase in population.

It would appear from Figure 10.1 that a GNPPC in 1972 of about $1,500 per year (under conditions of international trade) was the lowest GNP compatible with the reduction in infant mortality to the minimum level thus far observed, that is, 1.2 percent.[5] In 1972, Japan had the lowest level of infant mortality in relation to GNP (1.3 percent) at a per capita GNP of $1,430) while all countries with lower GNP had higher infant mortality. Similar low rates (1.25 and 1.33 percent) were reported from Finland and Iceland with fairly stable GNPs of $1,980 and $1,850 per capita, respectively, Sweden has the lowest IM in the world, 1.2 percent coupled with a low birth rate and a GNPPC of $2,920 per year. It appears that as the GNPPC moves above $1,500 per year, we see the beginning of affluence and the emergence of

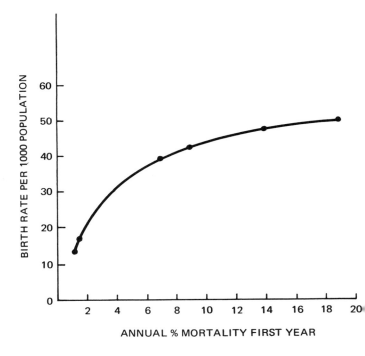

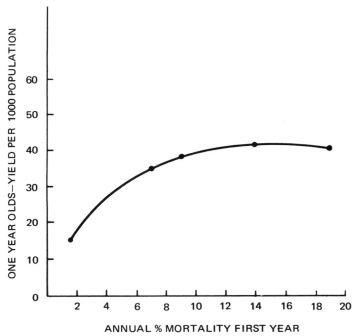

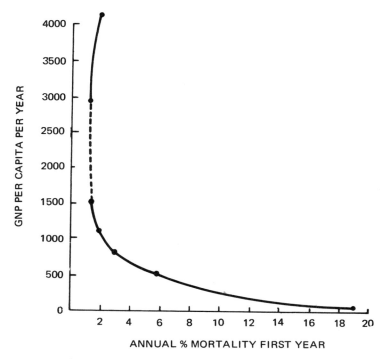

10.1. The Relationship Between Birth Rate, Infant Mortaility and GNP. The eight points on the graphs represent population data for eight different countries. The curves indicate not only the existing range of national GNPs, infant mortality rates and birth rates, but also represent the average of these factors for all nations. (Data from Population Reference Bureau, Inc.)

substantial segments of population which consume resources in excess of basic needs *without* any further reduction in IM. Thus the United States with a GNPPC of $4,240 in 1972 has not achieved a lower IM and in fact has a rate of 1.9 percent (Table 1.3. Chapter 1), somewhat higher than the rates in Sweden, Norway, Iceland, Finland, and Japan.

By using infant mortality as an indicator of equity in resource distribution, we are in effect asking whether the underdeveloped countries are condemned to their present high rates of IM until they are able to industrialize to the levels now seen in the United States and Western Europe or at least attain a GNP of $1,500 per year. The evidence suggests that this is not necessarily the case: it appears that not only did Japan have the lowest IM in relation to GNPPC in 1972, but it had similar low rates of IM at much lower rates of GNPPC in the two decades prior to 1972. The per capita GNP in Japan doubled to $1,190 between 1961 and 1968 (Table 1.2). Other data showed Japan to have reached a GNPPC of $1,430 by 1972,[6] while IM had been fairly constant over the entire period. Thus Japan may have achieved minimal

IM at GNPPC of $600 or less per year. This is of course much higher than the level of $100 or less seen in so many parts of Asia and Africa.

Further studies are needed to determine the cultural factors that enabled Japan to achieve a high health standard despite a relatively low GNPPC. It seems likely that a high level of literacy and respect for cultural traditions coupled with the shock of defeat in war produced the national policies for both effective birth control and infant and maternal health care. These policies were reinforced by a constantly increasing GNP.

It is not clear how the lessons from Japan can be applied on a global scale, since every culture has a different combination of traditions, resources, and world views. But it is clear that the kind of general health suggested by an IM of 1.2 percent is possible without the affluence of a modern United States or Sweden.[7] It is also clear that infant mortality is a useful social indicator for a biocybernetic technology aimed at achieving ideal survival.

Extreme variations in GNPPC within our own country lead us to inquire how resource consumption within each segment of the population is correlated with literacy, fertility control, infant mortality, and adult physical and mental health. There are many indications that some segments of our population could prosper with much less resource consumption although others are seriously deficient in material goods. In attempting to improve health, literacy, and overall ability in the so-called "pursuit of happiness" it seems important to combat the idea that these qualities increase in direct proportion to resource consumption. There is a certain minimal requirement for resource consumption in order to achieve the above goals as suggested by the Japanese record, but beyond that minimal level the increases may be counterproductive, as some of today's youth appear to have already realized.

Beyond the Minimal Requirements

After the absolute requirements for resource consumption (e.g., calories and protein) have been met, much can be accomplished by focusing more attention on *public goods* (mass transportation, parks, museums, schools, music and literature, experimental research) as contrasted with *private goods* (automobiles, clothes, small boats, snowmobiles, appliances). Carl H. Madden has commented:

> Private goods are those whose utility is determined by a person's exclusive possession and consumption of them. . . . Public goods, *once they are produced*, are not scarce in the same sense. One's enjoyment of them does not diminish another's ability to enjoy them, once they are produced. It is hard to grasp the astonishing impact of this idea, newly appreciated, for conventional marginal utility economics. . . . The entire concept of accounting . . . hinges on exclusiveness of use and destruction-in-consumption. Yet the wealth represented by public goods is simply not counted; it is a mystery. By the same token, accounting concepts in any balance sheet do not weigh the costs to a business of social deterioration in its environs or the accruals to a corporation of wealth from its environs.[8]

Further on, Madden speaks of what has in this chapter been implicit in the phrase "humanistically guided biocybernetic technology" when he refers to significant business opportunities that "await the transition of the corporation to the holistic mode" (a form that relates the parts to the whole). He suggests that

> in many aspects of world economic development, new and integrative outlooks will develop in the 1970's, offering new opportunities and strategies. In this new way of perceiving system, organization and process, the Cartesian view of products as parts which determine wholes will be supplemented by the holistic view that situations, patterns, configurations and wholes determine products.[9]

In other words, rather than developing new products that feed conspicuous consumption and that must be promoted to be sold, there is economic opportunity in developing services and products that meet the needs for environmental protection, public health care, and pollution prevention.

Advocacy of more public goods does *not* imply a limitless expansion in resource consumption as a means of achieving either equity or ideal survival. Rather, it suggests that there are tremendous possibilities for improvement in equity and human happiness, both within national borders and on a global scale, without the rate of resource depletion and energy consumption that present projections predict. Once the concept of "exclusiveness of use and destruction-in-consumption" is abandoned as a criterion of value, it should be possible to reexamine the GNP in terms of human needs and decide which items need reduction and which items might be expanded. Clearly, large blocks of the GNP will inevitably fall into the private sector (food, clothing, shelter) and require resource consumption. But constraints on private items that are superfluous and more attention to public goods could greatly enhance living standards without greatly increasing resource consumption. However, since millions have no excess, let alone essential, goods to give up, the first step must be to establish equity in the satisfaction of basic needs, an almost impossible feat in a population undergoing rapid exponential growth.

The Ethical Dimension

The mere consideration of the problem of equity implies that any kind of "ideal survival" must have a moral basis. In a world in which millions are condemned to a "miserable survival" many believe that those who are more fortunate are ethically bound to give some thought to the plight of those who are less fortunate. This ethical commandment has long been understood on an individual basis over most parts of the globe although the extent to which it governs behavior varies widely. What have never been made explicit are the ethical responsibilities between widely disparate cultures which may or may not share the same national boundaries. *On a finite earth, what are the ethical dimensions of a unilateral resource decision when the resource in question is localized within one or a few national boundaries?* What are the rights and responsibilities of a nation that has exceptional and surplus capabilities for food production? What are the rights and responsibilities of a nation that has surplus capabilities for oil production? What are the rights and responsibilities of a country that has inadequate capabilities in either food or oil production?

Each culture has developed in its own "ecological niche." Geography, climate, and intercultural exchange of ideas have interacted with the inventiveness of people to evolve cultures based on workable ideas. Many peoples adapted their cultures to the inhospitable geographic or climatic regions in which they had been forced to live by warring neighbors. Other peoples prospered and multiplied in favorable environments until exploding population, changes in climate, or depletion of the soil made it impossible for them to sustain themselves adequately. Then they either migrated to a new land or adapted their cultures to the new conditions. Most recently, wars, exploitation, and changes in the climate and the land have pushed cultures into circumstances in which their expanding populations cannot be supported in good health. But escape by migration is now impossible because of, among other things, immigration restrictions.

It is frequently argued that each nation has its own immutable cultural heritage, that its way of life is what it prefers, and that nations should not meddle with each other's lifestyles, even if vast populations are in obvious ill health. But it is sheer sophistry to maintain that their situation is merely the result of their cultural preferences, preferences with which others have no right to interfere. Foreign political-economic interests have already interfered and will continue to do so. Modern communications have moved into every corner of the earth. No culture exists in its pristine form. The ethical question in resource policy is how to develop a *morality of intervention*.

Any attempt to help underdeveloped countries or ethnic groups to understand their own plight; to move in the direction of adequate nutrition, shelter, and clothing; and to strive for a population size that is compatible with good health and with the local supply of resources is not an undertaking of "cultural imperialism" *as long as it is not exploitative*. The morality of intervention in the lives of individuals and nations is measured by the degree to which it is free from self-serving motivations in the *immediate* sense. Enlightened self-interest in the longer perspective is another matter and all attempts to achieve global idealistic survival are in the interest of every member of the human race.

In developing a morality of intervention we are here concerned with the deliberate intervention in the life of humans by other humans. We need not waste time on *malevolent* intervention since self-serving intervention that damages the recipient is clearly immoral. Much space could be given to categorizing and specifying various kinds of malevolent intervention, but what is at least as interesting is the ethical dimension of *benevolent* intervention, or literally, well-wishing intervention, since this goes back to the introductory section on "concerns and assumptions" in which it was pointed out that the best efforts may end in "unexpected and often unwanted consequences."

Seeking the Fine Line

In the case of benevolent intervention on an individual basis, the ethical problem is "to find the line that divides *professional service, friendship,* or *love* in any of its forms from the many custodial relationships that destroy human dignity."[10] On a global basis, the ethical dimension of resource policy decisions is similarly a fine line. On the one side, it can be argued that it is unethical to intervene, since each culture is totally responsible for its own future and deserves the kind of existence that its culture produces. Another view is that a people's culture is "their own affair," but their resources are "ours to exploit" by whatever methods can be arranged and at the least cost possible. In the vocabulary of power politics this may indeed be the idiom, and it should be rejected.

But western cultures also must avoid the other extreme, the arrogant assumption that they have all the answers and that their culture is the best possible form of human existence.[11] This attitude asserts that if other cultures would simply apply themselves and adopt western technology they would be as well-fed and mechanized as we are. This point of view leads to the most rapid kind of resource exploitation possible, all in the posture of benevolent intervention, but fraught with unexpected consequences.

Between these two extremes we have much to do. The present world operates on the basis of what is essentially intercultural and international social Darwinism, that is, a pragmatic survival-of-the-fittest philosophy in which hot wars, cold wars, and economic competition between nations have been a way of life. In this type of competitive struggle, technologists backed up by multinational corporations have responded with bigger, more intricate, and more costly machines, whether for war or for peace, thus speeding up the consumption of precious nonrenewable resources, while intervening in human lives and the natural balance of nature on a massive scale. Even if the threat of war and escalation of war technology could be diminished, the accelerated deployment of supertankers, superearthmovers[12] and super air transports would not diminsh the gap between the underdeveloped and the developed countries.

With recognition that we live on a finite earth, the need for an ethic that is not merely interpersonal but also global, intercultural, and environmental has become apparent. A paramount part of this ethic is that *all* nations, developed as well as underdeveloped, should be encouraged to maintain the capability to produce, with a low-energy technology, the renewable resources such as food crops, timber, and fish.

Another goal in the ethical dimension is the improvement of self-sufficiency, beginning with human health. To our knowledge there is no culture that places a premium on ill health. In the area of preventive medicine and public health, there are goals that all cultures can share, even while their philosophies may differ. However, it must be realized that as we export our progress in death control, we also must develop a complementary emphasis on birth control.

In pursuing the major goals of global health and self-reliance, idealists cannot expect to abolish intercultural competition, and should not attempt to do so. The fundamental position of benevolent intervention must be tempered by the biological truth that in diversity lies a basis for optimistic survival. Cultural diversity should be applauded and supported rather than homogenized. International trade will continue to be the lifeline of indigenous cultures all over the world. But in the ethical dimension, international communication and free dissemination of knowledge directed toward the twin goals of maximum human health and cultural self-reliance should be the key vectors. If these goals can be achieved without stifling the earth's cultural diversity, the evolution of cultures superior to any that now exist may be possible.

The chief obstacle to these goals, aside from the threat of war, is the tendency to use the vast machinery of communications for self-serving short-range objectives that attempt to increase the rate of resource consumption in ways that run counter to the concept of equity. The knowledge apparatus and the communications media thus become the battleground for forces seeking to influence the diverse cultures of the world. In the simplest terms, these forces are, on the one hand, arrogant, intrusive, and dedicated to the supremacy of a single culture. They hold an essentially military view of what is best for all the world's people, but have little apparent knowledge of biology, psychology, or ecology. These forces are not necessarily malevolent, but they are historically oriented and essentially pessimistic about long-range survival of most cultures. On the other hand, there are the forces that seek to encourage cultural diversity, and to preserve the natural life-giving forces of the earth. Such forces also can be arrogant and intrusive, but usually they are not. They tend to respect other points of view because of their inherent regard for diversity and for the vast complexity of environmental-cultural interaction. The contest between these forces represents an ethical problem, and thus raises the question of the individual's role.

The Role of the Individual

The knowledge apparatus and the communications media have just been referred to as key ingredients in mankind's struggle for survival. In the modern world, knowledge is accumulated by cooperative effort. As both J. Bronowski and Bentley Glass have pointed out,[13] building true knowledge is not a task for the introspective man who lacks access to libraries and laboratories. Yet facts, even when gathered by cooperative effort and with sophisticated apparatus, do not organize themselves. Men must do the critical organizing and evaluation. Recognizing the importance of this responsibility, Glass developed his four "commandments" for the ethical scientist which are, in summary:

1. To cherish complete truthfulness
2. To avoid self-aggrandizement at others' expense
3. Fearlessly to defend the freedom of scientific inquiry and opinion
4. Fully to communicate one's findings through primary publication, synthesis, and instruction

To this he added three responsibilities:

1. The proclamation of benefits
2. The warning of risks
3. The discussion of quandaries[14]

The points made by Bentley Glass seem to apply equally well to any participant in the modern knowledge apparatus, but especially to those in the rapidly developing field of environmental science. Individuals get ideas and insights, and propose hypotheses, theories, or laws. However, verification and approval by others, together with revision and reformulation, is a necessary ongoing part of the process. In other words, "knowledge is a social construct" and not a matter of individual divination. The process becomes complicated when the problems involve environmental-cultural interaction on a global scale, and when attempts are made to make resource policy decisions on a partly rational, partly intuitive basis that includes the ethical dimension.

We can only suggest that freedom of inquiry and free communications are paramount. Besides maintaining a posture of humility and respect for other points of view, those who support cultural diversity must be aggressive in their defense of open forums and the free dissemination of minority views.

What, then, is the role of the individual in this free flow of information? In the past it was said that "a man cannot serve two masters" and, again, "a house divided against itself cannot stand." In those days of restricted communication, strict allegiance to a single group was not only common but perhaps inevitable, except in the case of a very few individuals.

Cultural evolution in the direction of superspecialization in science, technology, and human affairs has been in part the modern expression of these ancient views.

But it might be suggested that much of the trouble in the world today can be traced to individuals who have sworn allegiance to a single group, a single company, a single discipline.

With widespread communications, it now is not only possible but desirable for many individuals to play active roles in two or more groups. In fact, the plethora of public and private organizations has generated a great need for individuals who have significant roles in several groups, because they can coordinate communication between often conflicting or competing points of view. Every individual who can contribute his particular expertise to the activity of two or more diverse groups has a tremendous opportunity to broaden his point of view and to look beyond the needs of a single group in a way that can contribute to the evolution and survival of the culture in which he finds himself. The role of the individual, then, in the development of global resource policy decisions would seem to be to test his beliefs and insights in dialogue with representatives of other groups, and to insist on their right to be heard, as well as his own.

Optimism and Pessimism

In resource policy decisions that have an impact on future survival and improvement of the human condition, there is a need to develop methods for dealing with the narrow point of view of specialists while at the same time utilizing their expertise.[15] One basic approach is the interdisciplinary group in which a diversity of viewpoints can be called upon.

Every discipline is regarded by its practitioners as a vital lifeline to the future and each views the world's problems a little differently. Engineers, agronomists, and technologists in general take an optimistic view of the future and follow the Churchill line: "Give us the tools and we will do the job." Some historians and philosophers take a more pessimistic view and regard the decline and fall of every culture as a fact of the past and an inevitability of the future. Biologists may argue for an evolutionary point of view in which nature selects the fittest civilization. But regardless of one's viewpoints, the realities of the need for adequate calories, adequate high quality protein, clean air, and clean water cannot be denied. The necessity for a world in which plants and animals can survive, if man is to survive, and the finiteness of living space and energy availability for the world population are all biological realities that affect everyone.

Thus in decision-making groups there is a need to incorporate competent specialists and then broaden their areas of competence by interaction with members of other disciplines. But there is also a need to develop an optimistic realism. In the words of Kenneth Clark, "Of course, civilization requires a modicum of material prosperity — enough to provide a little leisure. But far more, it requires confidence — confidence in the society in which one lives, belief in its philosophy, belief in its laws, and confidence in one's own mental powers. . . . Vigor, energy, vitality: all the great civilizations — or civilizing epochs — have had a weight of energy behind them."[16]

References

1.   Cf. discussion of the Godel Theorems by J. Bronowski: " . . . every axiomatic system of any mathematical richness is subject to severe limitations, whose incidence cannot be foreseen, and yet which cannot be circumvented," (J. Bronowski, *The Identity of Man* [Garden City, N.Y.: Natural History Press, 1971], p. 123).

2.   Carl H. Madden, *Clash of Culture: Management in an Age of Changing Values*, National Planning Association (Washington, D. C.: 1972), p. 47.

3.   Van R. Potter, "Disorder as a Built-In Component of Biological Systems: The Survival Imperative," *Zygon*, vol. 6, no. 2, pp. 138-39 (June 1971); see also Chapter 5, pp. 68-69, above.

4.   *World Population Report 1972*, Population Reference Bureau (Washington, D. C.), 1972.

5.   Ibid.

6.   Ibid.

7.   Similar conclusions, derived from the use of 24 socioeconomic indicators, have been reached in Charles Elliott, *The Development Decade* (London: SCM Press Ltd., 1971).

8.   Madden, *Clash of Culture*, p. 52.

9.   Ibid., p. 53.

10   Van R. Potter, "The Ethics of Nature and Nurture," *Zygon*, vol. 8, no. 1, p.41 (March 1973).

11.   As pointed out by C. N. Parkinson, there are two fallacies in this view: "The first lies in the assumption that all history illustrates a story of betterment or progress with ourselves as the final product. The second lies in the assumption that such progress

as there has been is a western achievement in which no oriental can claim even the smallest share." To this he adds that the view "is essentially pre-Darwinian as a mode of thought. No believer in evolution would expect to find that sort of finality." C. N. Parkinson, *The Evolution of Political Thought*, (Boston: Houghton Mifflin, 1958, Preface).

12. Such an earthmover is the "Gem of Egypt" which weighs 7,000 tons and can move 200 tons of earth in one scoop; James Conaway, "The Last of the West: Hell Strip it!," *The Atlantic*, vol. 232, no.1, p. 91 (September 1973). The cost of a similar machine, "Big Muskie," is estimated at $25 million; John F. Stacks, *Stripping*, (San Francisco: Sierra Club, 1972), p. 20.

13. For a discussion, see J. Bronowski, *Science and Human Values* (New York: Messner, 1956), pp. 72-74, and H. B. Glass, *Science and Ethical Values* (Chapel Hill, N.C.: University of North Carolina Press, 1965), pp. 82-84.

14. Glass, *Science and Ethical Values*, pp. 89-101.

15. Joseph R. Royce has stated: "What do we mean by encapsulation? In general, we mean claiming to have all the truth when one only has part of it. We mean claiming to have truth without being sufficiently aware of the limitations of one's approach to truth. We mean looking at life partially, but issuing statements concerning the wholeness of living." Joseph R. Royce, *The Encapsulated Man: An Interdisciplinary Essay on the Search for Meaning* (Princeton, N. J.: Van Nostrand, 1964, p. 30).

16. Kenneth M. Clark, *Civilization: A Personal View* (New York: Harper and Row, 1970), p. 4.

The Leonardo Scholars

WESLEY K. FOELL is associate professor of nuclear engineering and of environmental studies at the University of Wisconsin, Madison. He has conducted both theoretical and experimental research in nuclear reactor physics. His present work focuses on the environmental and systems aspects of energy production and usage. He has served as adviser to the Resources and Environment Program of the Ford Foundation and as chairperson of the Review Committee for the Experimental Breeder Reactor at Argonne National Laboratory. He is also adviser on energy matters for the state of Wisconsin and is a consultant to the Organization for Economic Cooperation and Development (OECD) in Paris.

PAUL G. HAYES is a reporter for the *Milwaukee Journal* specializing in public planning, natural resources, energy, and environmental issues. In 1968 and 1969 Mr. Hayes spent a year in Washington, D.C., observing Congress under the American Political Association's Congressional Fellowship Program. In 1972 he received the Gordon McQuarrie medal of the Wisconsin Natural Resource Foundation for conservation reporting. He is also a 1973 recipient of the Richard S. Davis Award for distinguished work by a *Journal* staff member.

MATTHEW HOLDEN, Jr. is professor of political science at the University of Wisconsin, Madison, specializing in American urban politics and public administration. Besides publishing many articles on a wide variety of subjects, he has authored a study of racial conflict entitled *The Divisible Republic* and has produced a monographic study, *Pollution Control as a Bargaining Process*. Professor Holden has served as a consultant to the mayor of Detroit, the U.S. Public Health Service, the National Academy of Science, and a number of other agencies. He currently holds a Presidential appointment as a member of the Air Quality Advisory Board.

JAMES B. MacDONALD, professor of law and of environmental studies at the University of Wisconsin, Madison, is coauthor of the books *Environmental Litigation* and *Water Rights*. He is a past director of legal research for the Environmental Defense Fund and was a coprincipal investigator for the Alaskan study of the Public Land Law Review Commission in 1967-1968. He served on the

Study Team on International Determinants of National Materials Policy, a joint project of the National Academy of Science and National Academy of Engineering. Professor MacDonald is currently chairman of the Environmental Law Committee of the Wisconsin State Bar.

VAN RENSSELAER POTTER is professor of oncology at the University of Wisconsin, Madison. In addition to numerous professional publications, including *Nucleic Acid Outlines* and *DNA Model Kit,* he has also authored *Bioethics, Bridge to the Future.* He is president of the American Association for Cancer Research and is a past president of the American Society for Cell Biology. Professor Potter received the Paul Lewis Award in Enzyme Chemistry in 1949 and the Bertner and Clowes Awards for cancer research in 1961 and 1964, respectively.

JAN VANSINA, currently on the faculty of the University of Louvain in Belgium, served as professor of African studies at the University of Wisconsin, Madison, from 1961 through 1973. Professor Vansina, a 1969 Guggenheim Fellow, won the Herskovits Award of the U.S. African Studies Association for his book *Kingdoms of the Savanna.* He also received the Belgian Royal Prize for History for his numerous articles on African history and anthropology. His most recent book is *The Tio Kingdom of the Middle Congo, 1880-1892.*

JEAN M. LANG, editor, is a science writer and editor with the Institute for Environmental Studies at the University of Wisconsin, Madison. She holds a B.A. in biology from the University of California and an M.S. in botany from the University of Wisconsin. *DENNIS L. FISHER,* associate editor, took a B.S. and M.S. in zoology as well as a law degree from the University of Wisconsin. He has worked with the pollution control unit of the Wisconsin attorney general's office.

List of Guest Participants

Participant	Major Topic Discussed	Affiliation
Eugene N. Cameron	Reserves of copper and other minerals	Professor of Geology, University of Wisconsin
Steve Hudson, Stan Flaum	Beverage container industry	Manager, Environmental Affairs, and Manager, Advertising and Public Relations, respectively, Continental Can Company
Robert C. Howell	Copper industry in Chile	Assistant Professor of Metallurgical and Mineral Engineering, University of Wisconsin
Theodore D. Tiemann	Copper processing	Professor of Metallurgical and Mineral Engineering, University of Wisconsin
John J. Sheehan	Labor unions in the copper industry	Legislative representative, United States Steel Workers
Stuart L. Cooper	Plastics as a substitute for metals	Associate Professor of Chemical Engineering, University of Wisconsin
Charles Michaelson, Herman Kremer, Edwin Dowell	Structure of the copper industry	President, Metal Mining Division, Vice-President, Metal Mining Division, and Director of Public Relations, respectively, Kennecott Copper Corp.
Meredith E. Ostrum	Mining in Wisconsin	State Geologist, Wisconsin Geological Survey, University of Wisconsin
Wesley Clayton	Environmental effects of SO_2 emissions	Past Director, Center for Environmental Toxicology, University of Wisconsin
Clancy C. Gordon	Environmental effects of SO_2 emissions	Director of Environmental Studies, University of Montana

Participant	Major Topic Discussed	Affiliation
John E. Kofron	Controlling environmental effects of power plants	Assistant Attorney General, Wisconsin Department of Justice
Peter Carstenson	Antitrust regulation of the copper and energy industries	Staff Attorney, Antitrust Division, U.S. Department of Justice
Charles Cicchetti	Economics of the oil and gas industries	Associate Professor of Economics, Associate Professor of Environmental Studies, University of Wisconsin
Sol Burstein	Problems and policies of electric utilities	Senior Vice-President, Wisconsin Electric Power Co.
William Eich	Administrative regulation of electric utilities	Chairman, Wisconsin Public Service Commission
Wolfgang Häfele	Analysis of nuclear material safeguard systems	Director, Institute for Applied Systems Analysis and Reactor Physics, Karlsruhe, Germany
Bruce Hannon	Systems analysis of energy requirements	Assistant Professor of General Engineering and Director of Energy Research Group, Center for Advanced Computation, University of Illinois
W. Donham Crawford	Energy policy position of U.S. electric utilities	President, Edison Electric Institute
Ed V. Goodin	Surveys and projections of oil and gas reserves	President, Petroleum Information, Inc.
Michel Potier	Attempts of a multinational agency to monitor and control environmental pollution	Head, Central Analysis Evaluation Unit, Environmental Directorate, Organization for Economic Cooperation and Development, Paris, France
Don Kanel, Burt Swanson	Institutional economics of agriculture	Professor of Agricultural Economics, Post doctoral student, respectively University of Wisconsin

Participant	Major Topic Discussed	Affiliation
Richard H. Day	Modeling economic systems	Professor of Economics Professor of Agricultural Economics, University of Wisconsin
Hazel L. Shands		Professor of Agronomy, University of Wisconsin
Harry C. Coppel	Integrated control of agricultural pests	Professor of Entomology, University of Wisconsin
Robert W. Houga	Genetics of crop plants	Associate Dean of Agriculture, Professor of Horticulture and Genetics, University of Wisconsin
Leo M. Walsh	Effects of fertilizer on agricultural soils	Professor and Chairman of Soil Sciences Department, University of Wisconsin
Fred H. Harrington	Agriculture in India	Former University President, Professor of History, University of Wisconsin
Reid Bryson	Climatic changes	Director, Institute for Environmental Studies, Professor of Meteorology, University of Wisconsin
Kenneth E. F. Watt	Systems modeling	Professor of Zoology, University of California, Davis
Roscoe E. Bell	Public and private development of Alaska's oil resource	Independent consultant on land and mineral resources
Henry Krebs	Population Trends	Research Analyst, Statistical Services Wisconsin Division of Health, Madison

Index

Adaptability: 18,19,148
Advertising: 8
Aerial photography: 30
Affluence: 9
Africa: 6
Air conditioners: 57, 92
Alaskan pipeline: 62
Aluminum: 106, 109, 112
Asia: 6
Atomic Energy Commission (AEC): 62, 64, 66, 80
Automobiles: 94-97, 113, 117

Battelle Memorial Institute: 37, 100, 106, 112, 113
Benveniste, Guy: 17
Biocybernetic technology: 142-143, 146
Biological resources. *See* Renewable Resources
Birth control: 19
Borgstrom, Georg: 8
Brownowski, J.: 150

Canadian Wheat Board: 35
Caribou: 29
Clark, Kenneth: 152
Classification of resource reserves: 26
Coal: estimate of resources, 26-28; formation of, 25; increased use of, 72, 74, 78; location of, 78; methods of extracting, 81; pollution from, 133-135, 138; solutions for problems concerning, 139; versus wheat, 74-80 *See*

also Strip mining
Collective farms: 20-21
Commoner, Barry: 4, 66
Common Market: 7
Consumer attitudes: 117-118
Copper: energy costs of, 102-106; essential uses of, 104-105; estimate of reserves, 25, 29; methods of processing, 102; pollution and disposal problems, 102, 135; pricing systems for, 31; recycling potentials for, 104-106, 113; as studied by Leonardo Seminar, xi-xii; substitute materials for, 105
Corn: 31
Cotton: 121-122
Crustal abundance: 24, 25

Data bank: 36-37
Decision-making: biophysical constraints on, 14; cultural constraints on, 15-19; estimates, projections, and forecasts in, 24-37; role of institutions in, 19-20; role of science in, 17
Department of Agriculture: 31, 76
Department of Interior: 24
Dimensions, time and space: 3, 6
Diversity: in biotic community, 2, 69; in energy use, 128-129; as part of "ideal survival," 143; in public attitudes, 17-18
Doubling time. *See* Exponential growth
Dubos, Rene: 61

159

Econometric model: 45-50
Economies of scale: xi, 119, 123
Education: 18
Electricity: alternative power systems for, 124-127; energy usage in, 8, 87; forecasting demand for, 46-49; in National Power Survey, 37-38; and nuclear power, 62-63; power failure, 122
Energy: alternative sources of, 124-127; conservation of, 90-102, 110; and materials flow, 85-89; research and development programs in, 123
Energy consumption: in copper processing, 102-104; in packaging, 107-109; in space heating, 90; in U.S., 123
Energy demand model. *See* Wisconsin State Energy Model
Energy-scenarios: 52-56
Environmental legislation: 8, 78, 128, 134-135, 138
Environmental Protection Agency (EPA): 100, 113, 133, 135
Equitable distribution of resources: 1, 143
Estimates: definition of, 23; dynamics of, 31; and projections, 33; role in resource policy, 24
Eutrophication: 61
Exponential growth: 3-4, 6, 8

"Faustian bargain": 63-67
Federal Agricultural Organization (FAO): 35
Federal Housing Administration (FHA): 92
Federal Office of Emergency Preparedness: 90
Federal Power Commission (FPC): 24, 37
Federal Power Survey. *See* National Power Survey
Feedback system: 42, 51, 142
Food and Agriculture Organization (FAO): 35
Ford Foundation: 120
Forecasts: 23, 33-37

Fossil fuels: 24, 123. *See also* Coal
Free market system: xii, 14
Fuel cells: 127

Geothermal energy: 124
Glass, Bentley: 150
Gofman, John W.: 63
Gross national product (GNP): 4, 42-43, 100, 143

Hannon, Bruce: 107, 109, 110
Health index: 7
Hierarchical systems organization: 43-44
Hirst, Eric: 92
Hubbert, M. King: 28
Huntington, Ellsworth: 15

Illinois: 78-80
India: 4, 18
Infant mortality: 7, 8, 143, 146
Institutions, social: 14, 19-20, 65-69
Insulation. *See* Space Heating
International Rice Research Institute (IRRI): 121
International Whaling Commission: 29
Interstate Commerce Commission (ICC): 112
Iron: 25

Japan: as adaptive society, 18, 22, 146; infant mortality in, 8, 143, 146; population growth and GNP of, 4

Kahan, Arcadius: 20
Kendall, Henry: 63
Kilocalorie: 11
Krill (*Euphausia superba*): 29
Kuwait: 25

Laird, Roy D.: 20
Land use: 30-31, 76-80
Lasky, S. G.: 25
Latin America: 6
Lead: 25
League of Women Voters: 111
Lewis, W. Bennett: 63

Limitation of growth: 1-4

Long-range planning: challenges of, 1-3; in energy use, 128-129; in land use, 82; need for, x; in reduction of pollution, 134

Lysenko, Trofim: 33

Madden, Carl H.: 146, 147

Marine fisheries: 72, 74

McKelvey, V. E.: 24

Mead, Margaret: 6

Meadows, D.: 3, 51

Mercury: 25, 33

Midwestern Corn Belt: 76-77

Mineral resources: 24-29. *See also* Nonrenewable resources

Models: 41-58; characteristics of, 43; criteria for evaluating, 42; definition of, 41; econometric, 45-46, 50; scenario, 50; simulation, 51

Montana: 78

Montesquieu: 14

Mount, T. D.: 38, 46, 47, 48

Moyers, John: 92

Myths: *See* Social myths

National Academy of Sciences: 118, 120

National Bureau of Standards: 90, 91

National Coal Association: 28, 133, 134

National Materials Policy Commission: 99, 106, 110, 112, 118

National Petroleum Council: 124

National Power Survey (NPS): 37-38, 57, 123

National Research Council: 120

Natural gas: 24-25, 28, 44, 127

Natural selection: 68

Nonrenewable resources: 24-29. *See also* Coal; copper

Nuclear power: 2, 62-65, 123

Oak Ridge National Laboratory: 38, 63, 90, 92, 102, 106

Oil. *See* Petroleum

Packaging industry: 107-110

Para-economics: 3, 10

Particulates: 133-135, 138

Pequegnat, W. E.: 29, 30

Pest control: 120-122

Petroleum: conflicts in use of, 74; location and distribution of, 25, 28; and pollution, 72; shortages of, 122

Pike River Claimants union: 14

Plant populations: 30

Plate tectonics: 33

Plutonium 239: 63, 64

Pollution: air, 132-138; government control of, 118, 134-135; point of no return, 9; related definitions, 140; science and technology in, 2, 4; sources of, 61, 72, 85-87; water, 132. *See also* Environmental legislation; Radioactive waste; Solid waste

Population: 2, 4, 6, 100

Potter, Van R.: 68

Power, in society: 16

Projections: 23, 34

Public opinion polls: 17

Quantification: 16-17

"Q unit": 87

Radioactive waste: 63-64

Ramo, Simon; 66, 68

Recycling: containers, 107-110; copper, 104-106; incentives for, 111-113; opportunities for, 87, 99-102

Resource conservation: 85-114; consumer awareness in, 118-119; of energy, 90-99; government control of, 118. *See also* Recycling

Resource consumption: future planning and, 146-147; historical perspective of, 12-13; risks and payments in, 60-62; by technology, 61; in U.S., 6, 8; versus population growth, 10

Resource policy: consumer attitudes and, 117-118; constraints on, 14-20; cost questions in, P2; environmental, 14; ethics in, 147-152; in industrial nations, xii, 10; long-range planning in, 1-2; qualities of, 2; science and, 17; society and, 13-14, 18, 114; in

underdeveloped nations, xii
Resource Recovery Act: 99
Resources: conflicts concerning, 72, 74-80; definitions of, 2; equitable distribution of, 1, 143; nonrenewable, 24-29; pricing policy of, xi-xii; renewable, 24, 29-31; transformation of, 85
Rice: 121
Rositzke: Harry: 20
Russia. *See* Soviet Union

Samuelson, P. A.: 34
Saudi Arabia: 25
Scenario-building: 50
Shortages: x, 62, 71, 100
Simulation models: 51
Skinner, B. F.: 66, 67, 68, 69
Social myths: 15-18
Solar energy: 125-126
Solid waste: 2, 107, 110, 138
Soviet Union: 6, 20-21, 33, 126
Space heating: 90-92, 124, 125, 127
Spaceship Earth: 1, 6
Strip mining: 72, 74-75, 78-81, 138
Subduction zones: 23
Sulfur: 72, 102, 133-137
Supernatural: 16, 21

Tamplin, Arthur R.: 63
Technology: 2, 61, 66-68, 86. *See also* Biocybernetic technology
Transportation systems: 92-99
Trend projection: 34, 44

United Nations (UN): 7

United States: coal resources in, 28; copper resources in, 29; energy and materials flow in, 87-89, 91-100; GNP, 4, 145; infant mortality in, 8; nuclear power in, 62, 65; population growth in, 4, 6, 100; shortages in, 71; social change in, 19; solid waste in, 110; strip mining in, 74; sulfur resources in, 137; total energy use in, 123; wheat farming in, 76-78
United States Geological Survey: 26, 28, 29, 78, 129
United States Senate Committee on Public Works: 99
Urban development: 76
Utility prices: 38

Values: in decision-making, 15-19; in long-range planning, 2; in resource policy, 147-152; in resource usage, 62, 72

Wald, George: 69
Ward, Barbara: 61
Wegener, Alfred: 23
Weinberg, Alvin: 63, 64, 65, 66, 69
Welfare economics: 18
Whales: 29-30, 39
Wheat: 74-80, 120
Wind energy: 126-127
Wisconsin: energy model, 51-57; energy use in, 92, 95-99; growth of electric utilities in, 45, 46; natural gas consumption in, 47
Wisconsin State Energy Model: 51-57